FRANCESC CATALÀ-ROCA

A PHOTOGRAPHER'S
IMPRESSIONS

RM

MEXICO / BARCELONA

Editorial RM

Editor-in-Chief
Ramón Reverté

Editorial Coordinator
Olimpia Nofuentes

Translated from Catalan by
Graham Thomson, 2025

Scan
Mahala Nuuk

Cover Design
underbau

Interior Design
Reverté-Aguilar

The translation of this work has been supported by a grant from the Institut Ramon Llull.

LLLL institut
ramon llull

RM #488-C

ISBN: 978-84-10290-13-6
DL: B 0024-2025

Printed in Spain
Liberdúplex; S.L.U.
Barcelona – España

Prologue

Francesc Català-Roca named his memoirs *"Impressions"*. It's a book of ambiguous genre, part autobiography, part philosophical glossary, part chronicle of events and character description. We can infer from the title that its author never abandoned his role as a photographer, as he is constantly describing "what he has seen."

It will not be difficult to recognize, in these narrated impressions, some of his most well-known images. But we will also discover others, rescued through literature, that the camera was unable to capture. The portrait of that time, which fits more or less with the author's well-known graphic images, will not be the defining feature of this narrative. Although it will certainly catch our attention, by offering us the author's experiential perspective on events, the most interesting aspect will be grasping the photographer's viewpoint on each anecdote, each moment, and each character.

This reflection emerges from the cultural background that nurtured the "Català-Roca phenomenon," the miracle of a dedicated photographer who documented fifty years of a country's life at the rhythm dictated by both his profession and his life. His principles are rooted in a combination of the traditions inherited from his rural childhood in the small agricultural town of Valls and the refined culture of the avant-garde during the Republic. He also learned hands-on in the laboratory, developing the contact sheets of the great reporters who passed through the Generalitat's Propaganda Commissariat during the Spanish Civil War. Later, in the postwar period, his relationships with the most interesting artists and intellectuals of the time also shaped his vision further.

For political reasons, the intellectual, and even ideological, legacy of these life experiences was not considered in reviews of his photographic work until much later. Today, we recognize the importance of this in understanding the solidity of his craft, the creativity of his style, and his ambition for modernity when editing and disseminating his photographs. Therefore, the "Català-Roca miracle," was really no miracle at all: it was not something that arose spontaneously.

On reading the text, his two defining influences will be evident: avant-garde theories and popular wisdom —paradoxical elements that define Català-Roca both in his photography and his discourse. Let us remember that in writing, the way things are said is as important as the content, the latter being rich in nuances, while the former is straightforward and brusque, much like the colloquial manner in which farmers discuss their affairs. His narrative is a testimony of turbulent times, where censorship and the prevailing moral standards of National Catholicism played a huge role in limiting freedom of expression, and because of this, humor and double meanings play a fundamental role in interpreting the text.

As for the photographs that illustrate this volume, they appear just as the author laid them out for the first edition. At first glance, these mosaics of images linking moments and characters resemble the contact sheets he used to manage his archive. Presumably, they also helped him sort through his memories while writing these memoirs.

Like other texts written by photographers, Català-Roca structures his memoirs as a glossary of aphorisms rather than a purely autobiographical account. His philosophical stance can be transparently superimposed onto each image he captured, bringing order —if more order were even necessary in his photography —to the world he left behind. A fragmented recital of ideas, sometimes contradictory, sometimes enigmatic, which both illuminate and obscure his thoughts on photography. To prevent the latter and allow light to continue illuminating the text, we must recognize his

I.
From Valls to Barcelona

Valls 1922–1931

Childhood memories are easy to forget, even though you realise that, from birth until the first years of conscious knowledge, many things will have happened to you, some of them important enough to be filed away in a corner of your memory, since they are the earliest ones that are seen or heard. I have a theory that, in much the same way as when you are aged six or seven you lose your milk teeth so that stronger ones can emerge, the brain is like a container that is constantly being filled and that sooner or later needs to be cleared out. I believe that at some point this clearing out occurred, but that some of my childhood memories must still be stored. What is certain is that they are all strongly rooted in Valls and, naturally, in the family setting. And very marked by the figure of my father. I was one of the 'kids from the portraitist's house'.

My father was the photographer (what used to be called a portraitist) in Valls. I was born on Carrer del Roser, at the corner with Carrer de la Cort, very close to the birthplace of two illustrious citizens of Valls: on the right, the home of Narcís Oller; and on the left, that of General Comerma. So, what are my earliest childhood memories? Well, I suppose they are not very different from those of other children, although some will be more specific to me, such as my memory of the days when I was woken by the sound of the *grallas* announcing the *castells*,[1] or that of the Dawn

---

[1] The *gralla* is a reed instrument typically played to accompany the *castell* 'castles' or human towers traditionally raised at festivals in certain parts of Catalonia, notably Valls.

Rosary procession, a typical manifestation of religious sentiment in that period, which would pass through the town early in the morning and was regularly jeered and booed by the bunch of anti-clericals who took part in the corresponding morning ruckus. Or my memory of the sound of the night watchmen gathering in front of the Town Hall before starting their nocturnal rounds, or the town crier with his trumpet announcing to everyone the proclamation entrusted to him (by the way, I encountered this figure of the town crier again, after the war,[2] in the streets of Cadaqués). Or my memories of the medicines that tasted so bad: the castor oil and cod liver oil, or the mineral water and the yogurt that we had to go to the pharmacy to buy. Or of getting new shoes, which in those days were made to measure, as were shirts. Or the month of Mary, which for me meant something out of the ordinary, since after dinner I went to sing in the choir at the Roser chapel, which was very close to home.

In fact, Valls was not very old at that time. But the Valls I knew best was the part of town between home and school. I set out from home on Carrer de la Cort to Plaça del Pati, from there to Plaça de la Font de la Manxa and then along Passeig dels Caputxins until I reached the Carmelite school, which I attended. Among all my memories, more than a few are centred on names and houses. For example, below our apartment there was a shop called El Figurí Infantil, which sold children's clothes, of course. Then there was the Moncunill bookshop: the Moncunill's had a large family, some of whom – the boys – went to school with me: Josep, Laureano and Joan. A little further on were Ca Sicart, the Centre de Lectura building, and the Màndoli tailor's, and on the other side of the street was the Can Nonian patisserie – so called because when we went there to buy I don't recall exactly what, they always said 'no n'hi ha' – 'there aren't any'. At Can Sanromà they sold anisette; speaking of which, I remember very well – from much later, in

---

[2] Unless otherwise specified, the war referred to is the Spanish Civil War.

Barcelona – that when people ordered this liqueur they would often ask for 'a glass of Valls'.

Some of the memories from that time are also associated with images that, back then, I would naturally have found quite startling, such as a Modernista building commonly known as Ca la senyora Tecleta, in which my sister Maria Àurea was born (it's curious how names like that have been dying out). Or the Valls cinema, built by Cèsar Martinell, which was the first in the town to screen sound films. A pharmacy, in front of which a small Citroën was always parked. A saddler's shop, which attracted my notice by the strong smell of leather that came from it. La Font de la Manxa, the pump fountain, so called because you had to turn an iron crank to make the water come out; and the petrol pump. The road to Montblanc started from this square, and it was here that my father suffered a small professional disappointment which he frequently recalled: it seems that the king's motorcade was to drive through this square on the way to Poblet or to Lleida, I don't remember which. So, my father positioned himself there to be able to photograph the king's car. But this was also precisely the place where the mayor and the town councillors were lined up. Of course, when the royal entourage stopped, my father took his photograph, but he could never use it because at that same moment the mayor held out his hand and in the print it looked as if he was sticking his finger in the king's mouth. Contretemps of the trade!

Another place where I used to stop, somewhat dazed, was at the bootmakers on Passeig dels Caputxins. I really liked watching them at work. Then came the library, the Biblioteca Popular, the first one built by the municipal association, and the Capuchin church, from where we would enter the school. I have an indelible image of this place: my sister Àurea giving a kiss to my younger brother, Pere, whom I accompanied to school from his very first day as a pupil, and the very long shadow they cast. Fifty years later, I returned to the same place, at the same time of year, at nine o'clock in the morning, and I realised that the incident light was what had provided me with the photographic image (without realising it at the time) of the elongated shadow cast by my brother and sister.

I also recall two significant events from those years: the first flight across the Atlantic by the aviator Lindbergh and the fall of the dictatorship of General Primo de Rivera. I remember the latter more clearly because my mother came to walk us home from school.

In any case, the most important memory is of the proclamation of the Republic and the series of events that in due course led me to understand politics. The most vivid record I have of that 14th of April (the day of the proclamation) is a photograph taken by my father showing the balcony of the Town Hall and the framed portrait of the king being thrown down into the square. In fact, I have another even more vivid memory: the tobacconist's shops back then used to have the flag of the monarchy painted on the door, and in next to no time they were all painted over with the Republican flag. We shall have more to say about those years later, but for now it is better to go a little more deeply into the many childhood memories that in time end up marking and conditioning – sometimes very much – adult life. In this light and somewhat in the line of the previous memories of places, houses and people, I recall a cafe that was on Plaça del Pati and was called La Unión Velocipedista, which must date from the introduction of that vehicle, the bicycle. Of course, in those days only wealthy people could afford to have a bicycle, a fact about which the Ramon Casas painting from Els Quatre Gats tavern of himself and Pere Romeu on a tandem is quite explicit. Speaking of money, I should also say that cycling was just as expensive as photography, and that only those who had the money to buy a camera could dedicate themselves to these activities.

Over the years I have become aware of several curious things about Valls. For example, I believe that at one point a wave of Italians arrived in the town, much like the one that arrived in New York and founded Little Italy! I think this may be so because there are quite a few families in Valls with an Italian surname:

Màndoli, Serafini, Mistieri… What rounds off my personal theory on this matter is that there was a municipality which went by the name – officially or otherwise – of Mesu, which in Italian means messenger or municipal officer. In fact, however, in Valls there are other surnames from different European countries, such as that of the Gherard family, from Switzerland, who gave important men to the country, one of whom, Robert, was a composer, and another, Carles, was a member of the Parliament of Catalonia and lay Commissary of the abbey of Montserrat during the Civil War. Their Swiss-German father had come to Valls for the wine trade, as the Müllers had in Tarragona or the Domecqs and the Osbornes in Andalusia.

Returning to my schoolboy memories of Valls, there was a woman who would come each day to walk several of us boys home after school. Oddly enough, although we were not allowed to walk to and from school alone, this rule was broken on Sundays to attend mass in the church of Sant Joan. I would go there with my brother Pere, and we were given ten centimes each to pay to have a seat, but in fact what we did was stand so as to save the ten centimes and buy an ice cream when we came out of mass. At that time, the first radios were beginning to appear, the galene crystal sets with earphones. The nuns who ran the school were given one, so we had the opportunity – one at a time after queuing for ages – to see and hear how this new means of communication worked.

The configuration of the town of Valls as it has stayed in my memory was made up of the urban core, plus the shacks, the *masia* farmhouses and the woods. The shacks – little houses on the outskits of town – were places of refuge for the workers on holidays and, of course, for the *calçotada*;[3] the farmhouses, the country retreats of the merchants or shopkeepers, the bourgeoisie; and, finally, in several places in the area known as El Bosc there were already some houses (villas) for, let us say, the upper class.

---

[3]   A *calçotada*, the communal char-grilling and consumption of the green onions known as *calçots*, is a custom which has spread from Valls to other parts of Catalonia.

Valls, then, where industry had developed, was clearly divided into different social classes. We rented a *masia* on the road to Montblanc, called Ca l'Esquilache, where we had a marvellous time. I remember that at the start of the summer holidays we would be bought two pairs of espadrilles, one for everyday wear and the other for going to mass on Sundays. That said, what usually happened was that after a while the first pair had been worn out and we ended up going barefoot everywhere. Since there was no electricity in the *masia*, we had to rely on carbide lamps for light. But the thing that has stayed with me most vividly is that whenever I was asked what I wanted to be when I grew up I invariably said 'a railway signalman'. This was due to the fact that whenever I passed the signal box I would invariably see the signalman under a vine with a pitcher of cool water next to him. An image that made me understand that this job was very tranquil – in those days the line carried no more than three or four trains a day – and very pleasant.

Valls–Barcelona. My mother

My mother hailed from Barcelona. She was born just in front of the cathedral, on Carrer de la Corríbia, a street which no longer exists. Her mother died in childbirth and her father placed her with a wet nurse and later at a school in Vic called El Escorial, a name that greatly impressed me as a boy until I learned that it meant nothing more than 'dung heap'.[4] At El Escorial she naturally made several friends who, when they left school, went back to their places of origin, many in Barcelona. When she married my father she went to live in Valls, of course, but she kept in touch with her two best friends from Barcelona, and every year she would make a trip to the city with me (because I was the eldest of her little brood). On our visits to Barcelona, we used to stay with a cousin of my mother's, my godmother, on Carrer dels Boters.

---

4   The standard sense of *escorial* is 'slag heap'.

Of my mother's friends, I remember two in particular: one lived on Rambla del Prat, where I discovered all the splendour of Barcelona (especially the grand houses!). This lady's name was Soldevila, and she was the mother of the actress Lali Soldevila. I must have been five or six years old then, and Lali had not yet been born, but I knew her sister, who was my age. One of the anecdotes I remember from those visits is that once, when I was in my best clothes, they wanted me to put on a girl's housecoat so I wouldn't get them dirty while playing, but I was so stubborn that I absolutely refused to wear it: so much so that I hid under the table. If they ask me now why I didn't want to put on that housecoat, the truth is that I don't know. I suppose it was because I didn't want to look like a girl. Sexist prejudice, it would be called now! My mother's other friend lived on Carrer d'Enric Granados. I really liked going to this house because I had a great time playing with a little dog they had. On next visit, a year later our, the first thing I did when we arrived was ask for the little animal, then they took me there and I found it under a table. The little dog was there, stock still with one paw raised, motionless. It had been stuffed and mounted! Since then, I have never been able to look at a stuffed animal.

I remember a couple of other things about these visits to Barcelona that disappointed me. One was going to the cathedral, which seemed smaller than the church of Sant Joan in Valls, and now I suppose it was because I was small, and the Choir prevented me from seeing the whole of the interior. The other big disappointment was that, when we walked down La Rambla, my mother used to say to me: 'Now we shall come to the sea.' But when we got to the Columbus monument, the only thing I could see was a huge pond – the port. The fact is I was used to looking at the sea from the balcony of La Rambla in Tarragona, all the way to the horizon! I think it was then that I began to have an idea of what images were.

Another thing I remember about my mother is that, in addition to being a lovely person, she was a wonderful mother to her three children. Since there were two women in our household, my mother and my grandmother, the so-called domestic tasks were divided: my mother took care of us children and her mother, like a good grandmother, ran the house. We really were a family in the fullest sense of the word: we always got on very well. There was only one little area of friction, which didn't trouble us too much, and that was that my father was not on the best of terms – I don't really know why – with his father-in-law. Grandpa Roca Sans died when I was still quite young. In any case, I remember that on one of our visits to Barcelona we went to see him. He lived on Carrer de Balmes on the corner of Carrer de Pelai and it was the first time I went up in an elevator! Before this he had been to Valls once, but he came to see us at school, not at home. Grandfather Ramon, who was also from Valls, was a university professor and lived for many years in Mendoza, in Argentina. When the phylloxera plague struck here, he was sent to Argentina to take grafts with which to save the vineyards of the Camp de Tarragona region. He was also a founding member of the Palau de la Música Catalana (by the way, there is a coat of arms very similar to the Austrian coat of arms, which is also that of Valls, in the parterre of the Palau, and I am almost certain it is there in honour of my grandfather). When he died, the Orfeó Català sang at his funeral in Barcelona cathedral. Francesca Bonnemaison, who was the wife of Narcís Verdaguer Callís and was the founder of the Institut de Cultura de la Dona, was my mother's godmother. As you see, practically all my family is from Valls, except the Pic branch, which was from Osséja in Pyrénées catalanes, and the Puig branch, which was from Barcelona.

Pere Català i Pic. My father

My father was a native of Valls, but when he was three years old he and his mother went to live in Barcelona. My grandmother, the widow Català, had lost her husband and two children in a single year. I know a few things about their stay in Barcelona: that they lived on Plaça de Sant Agustí, on Carrer Hospital, and on Plaça del

Beat Josep Oriol (now Plaça de Sant Josep Oriol) at the corner of
Carrer de la Palla. He went to a school on Carrer del Regomir,
the same school that Joan Miró also attended some years later, after
he had left. At the age of thirteen or fourteen, he started work as
a cashier in the Banco Hispano Americano, on Carrer de Pelai at
the corner of Jovellanos. In total there were about ten staff there
at that time, counting the manager. Of course, there were no
calculators then, so employees who knew how to count quickly
and accurately were highly valued. When my father would have
been about seventeen years old, the bank held a raffle for a folding
camera and he was the lucky winner. From that moment on, he
was drawn to photography. Before long, when he finished his day's
work in the bank he would go to the studio of the photographer
Areñas to help in the darkroom. One year when there was a great
snowfall in Barcelona my father obtained permission from the
bank manager to go out and take photographs of the wintry scenes.
When he turned twenty-five, and his age and years of experience
meant that he was ready to be promoted to manager, he decided
to leave Barcelona for Valls and go into business as a portrait
photographer.

At that time, most photography enthusiasts were rich people,
with significant purchasing power and also some knowledge of
chemistry and optics; these were considered to be 'photographers'.
The others, the professionals, were known as 'portraitists', because
it cost a lot of money to have a portrait painted by an artist and
only the wealthy could afford it, whereas photography was cheaper
enabled almost everyone to have a portrait of themselves or a
relative. These portraitists basically worked in three categories:
babies, first communions and weddings. A curious thing about
the baby pictures is that they were hardly ever taken before six
months, when the infant had begun to have a bit of character,
because established practice was to lay them on the floor, face
down, so that when the baby then raised his or her head to
breathe the photographer seized the moment to press the shutter.
First communions tended to take place, as now, in the spring. My

father used to keep in contact with the local priests, who would let him know in advance the days on which the ceremonies were held. And so every Sunday he would have to go to two or three towns to take the corresponding photographs. At first he went on a motorbike, a Harley-Davidson; then by car, a Renault. By the way, the local town crier used to communicate my father's visit in the following way: 'It is announced that on the day of the first communions the photographer Català from Valls will come to take the photographs.' And the crier used to add: '…which de does very well!' In 1931, when the declaration of the Republic was celebrated, a small boy told my father there would be very few communions that year. When my father asked him why, the boy answered, with all the innocence of his years, 'Because Our Lord has died.'

My father married Anna Roca i Puig in Valls in 1917, and they had a daughter and two sons: Maria Àurea, Francesc and Pere. In those years there was an artistic and intellectual movement of some importance in Valls. The brothers Jordi and Pau Mercader and the Gherard brothers lived there. I believe that my father must have found taking photographs of babies, communions or weddings increasingly difficult and tedious, since he was a very restless, enquiring man and keenly aware of what the future promised in the field of photography, especially in the fields of industrial production and advertising. This being so, in the very same year that the Republic was declared, he decided to return to Barcelona, where the opportunities to do new things were much greater. So the whole family moved to the city and my father began to work in the world of advertising, where almost everything was still in the form of freehand illustration. He enrolled in a course on advertising taught by a Russian named A. Chleusebairgue (whom my grandmother called Soler de Berga) at the Psychotechnical Institute directed by Dr Emili Mira. Afterwards, Dr Mira suggested that my father stay on to teach the Advertising Psychology course, which he did for two years even though he did not have a university degree and thus was not strictly qualified to do so.

Of course, when the Civil War broke out, the advertising industry ceased all activity, as did almost everything else. Dr Mira then introduced my father to Jaume Miravitlles, secretary of the Anti-Fascist Militia. My father was recruited to take the identity-card photographs of those being sent to the Aragon front. My father, who was always a hard worker, managed to do between 200 and 300 cards a day, which some of his colleagues reproached him for. It seems that even then Miravitlles was calling for the creation of a Ministry of Propaganda, which President Companys determined should instead be a Commissariat of Propaganda, under the aegis of the Ministry of Defence. Companys quite rightly decided to make this a Commissariat rather than a Ministry because it allowed him, on the one hand, not to have to appoint a new minister, which would have entailed negotiation with the different opposing parties, and on the other to exercise direct control of it himself. My father helped Miravitlles set up the new Commissariat, and once the idea was consolidated, the workers were asked to choose whether they wanted to stay at the Ministry of Defence or move to the new Commissariat of Propaganda. As my father was one of the prime movers, he opted to go and I went with him.

In the Commissariat, my father held the position of Director of Publications, the second most important after that of Miravitlles. He stopped taking photographs to hire photographers and illustrators for the production of books. This meant that he was working closely with Creixans, Clavé, Centelles, because everything published by the Commissariat came out of my father's office: books, magazines, brochures, posters… Naturally, he was also writing. I remember that he wrote the text for a story in pictures, 'The Auca of the humane anti-fascist Catalan boy',[5] with drawings by Obiols, and that my father did not sign it. His first secretary was a man called Monturiol who was a descendant of the inventor of the submarine. When Monturiol died during the war,

---

[5]   The auca is a traditional form of illustrated story, rather like a cartoon strip, popular in Catalonia and other parts of Spain from the 17th century.

his replacement was also from the Empordà, a son of the writer Josep Pous i Pagès. He also had as his assistant the writer Mercè Rodoreda, whom I remember very well. She was a wonderful woman and very brave. When she was working with my father, she won the Joan Creixells prize for her novel *Aloma*. I remember reading it and being very impressed.

A few days before the *nacionales* entered the city,[6] when everyone was preparing to leave or had already left, Francesc Pujols and Moraguetes came looking for my father, with a car that Pau Casals had left for them, to go to Prades. But my father, whose mother was very old and frail, was dead set against leaving. But as fate would have it, it was my mother who died a few days later, of pneumonia and the lack of medical attention, because there were no doctors. She was only 40 years old! To pay for her to be buried we needed fifteen of the old silver duros and we only had seven or eight. A good neighbour made up the difference. They came for her in a truck loaded with unpainted wooden coffins, which was collecting the dead house by house. Those who had no money to pay (since the currency of the Republic had been decreed worthless) had to keep their dead for days, which meant they had to air them on the balcony at night, until the cart came to take them away. We were told we should meet at Poblenou cemetery, where the dead were being taken. When we got there, all the coffins were lined up and had no lids. These are sad memories, marked not only by the pain occasioned by my mother's unexpected death but also by the circumstances that made everything much harder.

Having chosen not to go into exile, my father was forced to spend a couple of years without leaving the house under any circumstances. The political situation and the fact that he had been a senior official in the Commissariat of Propaganda made this advisable. As he liked to write he spent most of his time writing articles on advertising, art and photography. We were also lucky that the doorman of our apartment building was a good

---

6   The troops of the Movimiento Nacional established by Franco in 1937.

man and thought well of us, and on the various occasions when
he was asked for information about my father, he invariably
replied that he was a very fine person and had had nothing to
do with anything. Only on one occasion did they come up
to our apartment and on that occasion it was to ask my father for
information about Díaz-Plaja.

For my part, as I was a young person, and I suppose not
suspect in any way, I continued to work in the new department
that was created with the arrival of the so-called *nacionales*. The
writer Ignasi Agustí also worked there, and he asked me to stay to
run the offset machine. At that time, I was paid the same as a tram
driver: seventeen pesetas a day. My brother Pere had to leave school
and started working at the Banco Hispano Americano, as first my
grandfather Roca and then my father had done, where he earned
two hundred and seventy pesetas a month. The family lived on
these two wages. Pere left his job at the bank when I set up on my
own and took over from me as father's assistant. My father, after
this long parenthesis, had returned to photography and I did the
jobs that he didn't want or couldn't do.

As I have pointed out on other occasions, my father was
a self-taught man in practically everything, with a boundless
curiosity and a great ability to adapt to the changing times (in
every sense). He was a cultured man in the broadest sense of the
word and a lover of poetry, to such an extent that even as children
he read us a lot of poetry. Maragall, García Lorca, etc. Although
we went to mass every Sunday, he was not particularly religious –
he was a man of the centre, Catalanist and republican. He mixed
with with the leading Valls intellectuals, such as the Mercaders,
the Gherard brothers, Màndoli… He could have been shot, as
Carrasco i Formiguera and Planes were. As well as intellectuals
and politicians, my father had other good friends, such as fellow
members of the Publi Club, an association of advertising people,
which included Prat Gaballí, Barnils and Aubeisson.

My father's friends in Barcelona were mainly artists,
intellectuals and so on directly or indirectly involved in the arts.

So I can talk about some of my father's friends, such as Prats (friend, champion and patron of many artists), and Josep Lluís Sert, with whom I naturally kept up a long friendship and professional relationship. To these names I should add all those people who were linked to different artistic movements or currents, such as GATCPAC (mostly architects) or ADLAN (primarily artists). These were very progressive people in every sense, and when the Civil War was over and General Franco's troops entered Barcelona they had to mute their activities; the groups as such ceased to exist, and many of them their later life was spent in exile. This inevitably resulted in a major reverse in terms of artistic innovation and a return, above all in architecture, to the Neoclassicism so beloved of the fascist movements then dominant in much of Europe and as such a major influence within Francoism.

My father wrote reviews of photographic exhibitions for magazines such as *El Mirador* and *Ford*, and thanks to his friendships and connections in these groups, so influential in the artistic context, he was among the first to be acquainted with various international figures in a variety of fields. So it was that, through my father's work, I was able to get to know the photographic work of Man Ray, for example, much earlier than most other people. My father's knowledge of these artists' work provided me with a great cultural and professional background subsequently mentioned in several articles. To illustrate this, it is worth reproducing a short piece by Jaume Miravitlles about the Commissariat of Propaganda which appeared in *La Vanguardia*: *The Graphic Documents section was set up at this time, with the titles of the photographs in Catalan, Castilian, French and English. The monthly magazine called Nova Iberia was also published in Catalan, Castilian and Galician. Its creator was* PERE CATALÀ, *creator of the famous poster in which a Mosso's foot is shown breaking the sphinx of the swastika.[7] We can now reveal a circumstance that may seem innocent but that at the time was very dangerous: the*

---

[7] The Mossos d'Esquadra, known informally as Mossos, are the autonomous police force of the Generalitat.

Now that a good number of years have passed, when I reflect on all these things, in many of which my father was involved, I realise how little time he had to devote himself to photography, which is what he really liked best. In any case, after the war was over he always found some more or less plausible excuse to take the occasional photo. With regard to this I remember the time we went Jerez together to take some photographs, which was my first long trip. I also realise that the fact of having an intelligent, cultured father, interested in everything and everyone, even though self-taught, is a spectacular advantage for his children – in this particular case, for my sister, my brother and me. In other words, we had a great advantage from the start. We owe all that we are to him, especially the good education he knew how to give us.

When he gave each of us our first camera, he made us promise in writing that we would learn how to use it and take good care of it. This encouragement to take responsibility for our own things was to prove crucial for our further development as persons and as professionals. All three of us, then, started in photography, although my sister chose to study drawing and subsequently went on to teach the subject. She even had an exhibition at the Ateneu Barcelonès, and though she was not a great artist, she did have a real talent for drawing. She never married and lived with our father until he died. My brother, on the other hand, did marry, into a family with close links to the world of art, his wife being the Valencia-born granddaughter of the gallery owner Dalmau.

First works in photography

In 1935 I asked my father if I might leave school and start working in his studio. He agreed in part, in that he made it a condition of working with him in the mornings that in the afternoons I should go to the Acadèmia Cots on Portal de l'Àngel; and so, when I was just thirteen years old I became a professional photographer. One of the first jobs I remember was helping to make a photomontage for the Maryland cinema for the film *A Midsummer Night's Dream*. In reality, however, what I mostly did was accompany my father, helping to carry his suitcase full of photographic equipment. For instance, I remember accompanying him to the Sala Esteve (later called the Sala Victòria) on Carrer de Casp at the corner of Pau Claris. On that occasion we were going to take the photographs of the latest Picasso exhibition there, shortly before the war. On another occasion I remember going to the Nobel Hotel on Carrer de Santa Anna to photograph the French poet Paul Éluard, who had come to give a talk at the opening of the Picasso exhibition.

I also remember going to a gallery where paintings were on show, where I heard about the scandal surrounding *El vi de Kios*, the painting for which Pere Pruna had been awarded the Isidre Nonell prize at the Saló de Montjuïc in 1936, and which he had apparently copied from a photograph in the magazine *Sex Appeal*.

The fact is that my first beginnings as a photographer coincided almost exactly with the outbreak of the Civil War. For this reason, my memories of that time are closely related to all that happened in the previous period and to the subsequent revolt and outbreak of war. With the monarchy still in place at the end of the twenties, the International Olympic Committee had awarded the hosting of the 1936 Olympics to the city of Barcelona. But in 1931 the monarchy was replaced by the Republic, and the organisers, most of whom were monarchists, lost their positions. This, added to Hitler's rise to power in Germany and his interest in using the

worldwide repercussion afforded by the Olympic Games to benefit
his propaganda apparatus, led the IOC to change its decision and
end up transferring the responsibility to Berlin.

Obviously all the democrats and anti-fascists disagreed
with this, and as a result a People's Olympiad was planned, to be
inaugurated on 19 July 1936 in the Montjuïc stadium, and many
of the athletes from the various delegations responded to the
dramatic events by enlisting in the militias. The column which was
sent to defend Zaragoza thus became the basis of the International
Brigades. I remember that a salvo of mortar shots had been
scheduled for the nineteenth of July, the day of the inauguration
of the People's Olympiad… and shots there were, indeed, but of
a different kind! I could hear them from our apartment. That
afternoon, from our balcony I saw a boy in Plaça de Cucurulla
with a pistol in his hand who made everyone that passed in front
of him raise their arms. A little later I noticed how quiet it was and
I went out, intending to go to Plaça de Catalunya; when I came to
the corner of Carrer de Duran i Bas and Portal de l'Àngel I saw
a tailor's shop with its frontage smashed. The Republicans had set
up a 7.5 cm cannon to fire at the Hotel Colón, and the recoil had
hit the display window! The first thing that struck me on arriving
at Plaça de Catalunya was the sight of dead horses and donkeys
(the dead people had already been removed). The animals were
left there for several days, and the stench became unbearable. To
counteract this, until they could be removed, they were doused
with disinfectant (even now the smell of disinfectant always
reminds me of the nineteenth of July). Quite soon, my memories
of the first days of the war came to associate these images with the
sight of photographs of human corpses, of captured soldiers… One
of these photos shows a militiaman in front of the Hotel Colón
(now the Banesto bank), stripped to the waist and with a machine
gun in his hands – that very vivid photo must have been taken by
Centelles. Other images, also very vivid, are of the storming of the
Episcopal Palace on Plaça Nova. The militiamen inside the Palace
had put on chasubles and were throwing pieces of furniture out of

the windows onto the square, where another group of militiamen
were enthusiastically destroying them… El Montepío, on Plaça
de Sant Jaume, was where people went to pawn their possessions
for cash, and on the day the order was given to return all the
pawned objects a queue of happy people formed. These were the
protagonists of an unusual spectacle. For example, a man would
come out with a mattress on his head, someone else had a bass
drum and was banging it… Some people would have recovered
their jewellery but you couldn't see it because they had it in their
pockets. It's a pity I couldn't take any photos, but I have kept all
these images impressed in my mind, like the one a few days later
in Plaça del Bonsuccés, where I saw a piano propped against the
railing of a second-floor balcony tilting forward until it slid off and
fell with a resounding crash into Carrer d'en Xuclà.

II.
The civil war

The commissariat of propaganda

The vision I have of the Civil War is above all visual, photographic, and that of a young person who, by virtue of his youth, experienced it in a context that was political but not politicised. I say this in the sense that what I did was to follow my father and I therefore lived, saw and understood the war through my father's work and personal relationships. In fact, before delving into specific aspects of the Civil War, I would like to give my particular view. The months that followed the military insurrection of July 1936 were key for the Republic to lose the war.

The *alzamiento* had failed everywhere except in Seville,[8] but as a result of that fact the Republican political parties, instead of uniting to form a common front, began to fight among themselves. Meanwhile, the leaders of the military coup, perceiving their failure, met and united in Salamanca to appoint a single commander. It seems that the choice was to be between two generals, I think they were Cabanellas and Mola, but when they were unable to agree on which they decided that the position would be occupied provisionally by a young general named Franco, who would be replaced in due course. They never managed to replace him, and Franco became the *Generalísimo*. The first thing he did was to bring together the different parties or tendencies that sided with him to create the Falange Española de las Juntas de

---

[8] Literally, a revolt or rebellion: the military coup of July 1936 against the Republican government.

Ofensiva Nacional Sindicalista [Spanish Falange of the Councils of the National Syndicalist Offensive]. The unity and direction demonstrated by these Nationalists earned them Hitler's approval and he granted them total aid.

After the battle of Teruel, Prieto, who was the head of the Republican government, was convinced that the war was lost and resigned. His successor, Negrín, also saw the war as lost, but he took the long view, since there was a palpable and widespread feeling that what was coming would be a conflict on a European scale that would force the non-fascist countries to abandon their neutrality and intervene. Negrín came up with the slogan 'To resist is to win', and truth is that if the Republic had held out for just six months more he would have been proved right.

Let us return now to Barcelona in July 1936. The military rebels were eliminated and the Anti-Fascist Militias were created to fill the void and defend the interests of the Republic, but unfortunately there were also so-called *incontrolats*, not necessarily aligned with any ideology. These uncontrolled elements did as they saw fit, including *paseos* and other savage acts,[9] and to control them Companys created a Conselleria de Defense: a Ministry of Defence with soldiers loyal to the Republic. My father and Miravitlles, who were working with the Militias in the Institut Nàutic building on Pla de Palau, were transferred to the new Ministry of Defence headquarters in the Capitania building on Passeig de Colom, where not long after I also went to work; I was fourteen years old at the time. The Saló de Sessions hall there had been partitioned into compartments and one of these was occupied by the photographic archive, where my job was to sort and file the photos that arrived from the Aragon front; as I said before, my contact with the war was basically visual.

Among my strongest memories of that time, then, are many of those photographs and some of the people who worked or frequently passed through there. For example, one of the photos

---

9   In this context a *paseo*, literally a walk or stroll, is an execution without trial.

that impressed me the most was of a pond with a dozen Civil
Guard tricorne hats floating in the water. I also clearly recall an
office with a sign that read: 'This is the office of Comrade Llano
de la Encomienda.' He was the Captain General of Catalonia
whose refusal to join the coup obliged the rebels to bring Goded
from Mallorca. I saw him a few times, accompanied by General
Aranguren, who was then head of the Civil Guard, both of them
dressed in green overalls… By the way, Aranguren was shot by
order of Franco when the *nacionales* entered Barcelona. One day
a personage of the category generally called important appeared
in the photographic archive. Posters had been printed with his
photograph on them, which I was in charge of keeping, and he
told me to give him a few. I made him a package and he very
kindly thanked me. It was Durruti, who not long after was killed
in the Battle of Madrid. Incidentally, the photograph on the
poster was by Agulló. Some of the other photos that had a strong
impact on me were by Tarragó, who was my direct superior
in the archive. One of them was a photograph of dead bodies
from the Arrabassada, the corpses of people who had been taken
for a *paseo*.

During my time in the Capitania I made a good friend. He
was a militiaman, and eighteen, so he was older than me – I still
wanted to play more than anything else, and he was the object of
my desire to have fun and generally make mischief. As a result, we
became great friends and he always told to me what he was doing.
Once, when I arrived at the Conselleria a little later than usual, I
found him happier than ever. He told me that in Poble Sec, where
he lived, for the past few days there had been a 'Paco' (the name
given to the snipers who would fire in the air to create a sense of
insecurity) whom the militiamen had been trying to catch for days.
As my friend was leaving his building to come to the Conselleria,
he heard a shot and saw a flash from a roof very close by. He ran
straight to it, grabbed the man, lifted him on his shoulders and
threw him down into the street. He was very happy telling me this,
because he had done his duty, and I was thinking that what he had

done was to kill someone. However, I did not stop being friends
with him on that account.

One day, my father told me that he had to make a poster
and told me to go to Carrer dels Tallers to get some clay, which
he needed to make a swastika. I modelled the swastika myself and
mounted it on wood. We went to the entrance of the Capitania
and, at the door on the left facing the façade we prepared the scene
to take the photograph. It was at night. We placed a chair and I wet
the cobblestones in front of it. Then we set up a spotlight on it,
laid the swastika on the ground and sat a *Mosso* on the chair with a
rifle between his knees so that he wouldn't move. We got him to sit
in such a way that he seemed to be crushing the cross with his foot,
and took two 13 × 18 cm plates. The result was one of the most
famous posters of the Civil War. And one of the most innovative,
as this was one of the first posters in the world made from a
photograph instead of a drawing or a painting. A poster which had
no need for any text, as the photograph spoke for itself. That said,
there were two things about the final poster that my critical sense
was not quite happy with: one, that it had a mount, and the other,
the unnecessary caption 'We crush fascism', which ended up being
included. In addition, circumstances or printing limitations meant
that the graphics studio that produced it had to make it in two
parts due to the size of the poster: 80 × 100 cm. However, Dalmau
Oliveras, the printers, did such a good job that the split was not at
all noticeable. By the way, Dalmau Oliveras was a very good and
very important hardware store, in which Miró worked for a while.
The firm had a graphic arts workshop on the corner of Carrer de
Londres and Casanova, which is where the poster was printed.

At this point, I cannot refrain from reproducing a short
excerpt from an article by the Russian journalist Ilya Ehrenburg,
who was a correspondent during the Civil War, published in the
Crónica general de España collection. With reference to Barcelona, he
wrote, among other things:

*I saw Barcelona again. The extraordinary clarity of autumn
invested even the florists' kiosks on Las Ramblas with a hint of wisdom.*

In fact, memories very often tend to be scattered, which is why, as I set down details of the specific period of the war, they come back to me under this condition. I now recall the first time I had the feeling that things were not going too well. That day, when I arrived at the Capitania, I found the yard full of militiamen who had just come from Mallorca; they looked very tired, dirty and downcast… This was the first symptom of a future defeat. I also clearly recall the day that Miravitlles came from the Palau de la Generalitat with a lot of signed papers and told his secretary —a big tall fellow with a pistol at his waist, called Requena— to go at once to requisition premises in which to install the offices of the Commissariat. Someone, I don't remember who, suggested the Palau Robert on Passeig de Gràcia. A few hours later, Requena came back saying that we now had new premises. 'The Palau Robert?' someone asked. 'No,' he said, 'but just across the street. When I tried to enter the Palau Robert, an old man told me that we would only get in there over his dead body. I mean to say, what was I to do?' So concluded the tall, heavy set man with a gun in his waistband. Paradoxical, surely?

There we met a great number of journalists, some of those who had in fact been sent to cover the People's Olympiad but, finding themselves in the middle of the conflict, decided to stay in the city to report on the war. I became very friendly with the correspondent from the Russian newspaper *Pravda*, Owadja Kuperman. It was he who taught me to play chess, and he was a first-class player (he had even played the world champion, who was the Dutch champion Euwe). I remember that when I made a bad move, he would taunt me by calling me 'bishop'! Owadja ran into a big problem: he had no typewriter. Not because there were none, but because those that we had were not in the Cyrillic alphabet.

Naturally, the Commissariat wasted no time in arranging with the Underwood company to ensure that the *Pravda* correspondent was able do his job as well as possible. I was sent to pick up the new typewriter from the company's premises on the corner of Ronda de la Universitat and Carrer de Balmes. Problem solved for Owadja… But not for me, because we had only a few typewriters left, and there was always some smartass who took the Cyrillic one and, when he realised what it was, would just leave it in some office or other. One of my chores was to seek it out and return it to its regular –and only– user.

It goes without saying that at that time all the world's press took note of what was happening in Spain. When this happens, there is always some chancer who tries to take advantage of the situation. In this case it was the actor Errol Flynn. One fine day he turned up at the Commissariat and a man was assigned a person to show him around. When this fellow returned he told us that Errol Flynn was an idiot, because he had asked to have his photograph taken with a group of militiamen dressed in white sheets. Thinking over this strange request, it occurred to me that Flynn had made a basic geographical blunder. He must have thought that he was in Abyssinia, where there was also a war. Another of the important people that I remember most from those days is Paul Robeson, whom I already knew about before the war, having seen him in some film or other at the Maryland cinema. The famous singer and actor sang 'Els segadors' in the Gran Teatre del Liceu.[10] The great pity is that there is no recorded evidence of that memorable occasion when the great Black bass-baritone sang our national anthem.

In addition to working with my father, I was an assistant to the photographer Josep Sala. My job, as it had been with my father, was to carry the case with all the equipment. One day we had to go to the Palau de la Generalitat to take a portrait of President Companys, which would later become the official photo. Another

---

10   'Els segadors' –The Reapers– is the official national anthem of Catalonia.

day we were sent out to photograph the British fleet, which was anchored outside the port. Sala, who was rather a timid fellow, confided in me that he was a little anxious because he didn't know how the British sailors would react if they saw us photographing them. I told him it was very unlikely that they would shell us and he replied: 'Maybe not a shell, but they could blast us with the "death ray".' Another recollection of my work with Sala is a trip to the Hospital de Sant Pau to photograph a militiaman considered to be a 'hero', who had been wounded on the Huesca front (it seems that this militiaman was the only one who dared to go alone as far as the cemetery there). He was in bed, surrounded by family members, who were happy that the wounded man was recovering. Beside the bed was a chair that served as a bedside table, on top of which were his wallet, his papers and a pile of coins. The family scene ended when one of the hero's young nieces bumped into the chair, knocking everything off it, and the girl's father gave her a good slap. The hero, naturally, defended her. Hanging over the back of the chair was a pair of green trousers; someone said something about them and I remember, as if it were this very moment, the militiaman's reply. The trousers had belonged to a Civil Guard lieutenant whom they had shot. 'Our hero', realising that the man was the same size as him, made him take off his trousers before they shot him so as not to spoil them. And there they were! The poor lieutenant was shot in his underpants! That wretched war...

Another occasion on which I accompanied Josep Sala was to take some photos at the Russian consulate on Avinguda del Tibidabo. We took the group photo after the lunch served at the conclusion of an official meeting, and while we were gathering up our stuff everyone went out and left us alone in the dining room. There were silver sugar bowls on the table and I remember tipping the contents of one of them into my pocket –however, I left the bowl on the table. This makes me think that in the matter of food, things were starting to get difficult.

As we are on the subject of Russia, let me mention that one of the most important episodes of the Revolution was the storming of the Winter Palace in Saint Petersburg, a fact that I knew from an important film by a great director whose name I do not remember, which recreated the events with many of the actual participants appearing as themselves, and the most important of these was Antonov-Ovseenko, who duly became Russia, consul in Barcelona and whom we had the opportunity to photograph as I have explained.

One day, Mr. Antonov-Ovseenko read in the newspaper *Pravda* that he had been appointed a Commissar in the government, and he went back to the USSR to take up his post. What he did not know was that he had been given a unique copy of *Pravda* specially printed to entrap him, and onhis return to Russia he was shot. A man who had been one of the greatest heroes of the Russian Revolution fell victim to Stalin's purges.

As the war dragged on, it became more difficult to get groceries. The supplies department gave us vouchers that entitled us to have lunch at one of the 'popular restaurants'. I enrolled in one called Rugby, on the corner of Pau Claris and Consell de Cent. Every day they gave us the same menu: rice with lentils, fish and an apple. The only thing that changed every day was the bill of fare. One day it said 'Rice with lentils', another 'Carmelite rice', and another 'Mixed legumes'… There was no shortage of inventiveness. After the war was over, I found out that many of the customers I used to meet there every day were priests. Having lunched at the Rugby, for dinner I used to go to the Association of Generalitat Employees, which was in an apartment on the corner of Passeig de Gràcia and Aragó. I used to go there because I could eat my not only my share but also what my colleague Labielle gave me in exchange for my bottle of wine. So, on some days I ate three meals. I was then sixteen years old. On occasion, in order to get something else to eat, I would cycle out to the Can Bach farmhouse in Sant Esteve de Ses Rovires. There, in exchange for caustic soda, which I procured from the Commissariat paper factory, which they used to make soap, they gave me two litres of milk, a rabbit and a dozen eggs. What more could anyone ask for?

The bombardments

At the start of the war, the authorities tried to prepare us for the possibility of being bombed. They did this by telling us about the bombing from the air in China —up until then the only shelling had been by cannons and from the ground. We were told that the sirens would sound a first warning and that when we heard them we were to take shelter in a basement or, failing that, on the ground floor. Strips of paper were to be stuck to the windows so that the blast did not shatter the glass in pieces. At home, when the alarm sounded, we went down to the main floor of the house on Carrer del Pi at the corner of Portaferrissa where we lived. This was the apartment of the owner of the building, Sr. Modolell. At first, the alarms turned out to be false. But I remember —it is hard to forget— the first time we endured the effects of a bombardment. We were in the shelter, of course, but even so we could hear the whistle of the projectiles being fired from the cruiser *Canarias*; later we learned that one of the shells had hit a house on Carrer del Perill, in Gràcia. The impacts of the shrapnel can be seen even now. Rumour had it that the intended target had been the Elizalde factory on Passeig de Sant Joan, where they made engines.

Another bombardment that I remember very clearly took place one day around noon. I was working at the Commissariat when the alarm sounded and a split second later I heard a very dry crack. We were starting to get used to the shelling by then, and we could tell if the projectile had exploded nearby or farther away. When I heard the alarm I went out towards Diagonal and saw a plume of smoke in the direction of Passeig de Sant Joan. I started running and when I got to Carrer de Roger de Llúria I saw a man covered in blood. The shall had fallen at the corner of Diagonal and Bailén. It was already winter, but as it was a nice day lots of children had been out playing in the sun. I still recall that there was a farrier's on the corner; there were pieces of horse flesh sticking to the walls and some men were scraping them off and wrapping them in blankets. It was horrible! But what seems even more horrible now is that, having witnessed those scenes, I went off to lunch because it was time to eat. The truth is that when I think about it, when I reflect on my behaviour at the time, I don't know whether I was in shock, whether I was unconscious or whether, since I could have been one of the dead, the sheer contentment at being alive had rendered me insensible. In fact I tend to think that as horrors become everyday they make you insensitive; they harden you to such an extent that, when you are not directly affected, they fail to move you.

The most significant of the air raids that I remember, however, is the one in which a bomb landed on the corner of Gran Vía and Balmes, demolishing several buildings. It was quite staggering. Indeed, it later became known that the Germans had used us as guinea pigs, trying out a type of bomb which they went on to perfect and use against British cities. I also remember the bombing raid that hit Sant Felip Neri square. The church there was giving shelter to war refugees, and the girls and boys used to go outside to play. One day a bomb was dropped on the square, killing at least fifteen children. If you go there even now you will still see quite clearly the impact of the explosion on the pitted façade. In view of all these facts, my father decided to move away from the city centre. As one of his friends, who was a cousin of the Minister of Public Works (the Valencian, Juli Just) and lived on Avinguda del Tibidabo, we moved there. So it was that we went to live in a very large mansion, which we shared with many other people. One of these was the writer Blasco Ibáñez's sister, who was married to a man named Carsi. Another was a man called Poll. Regarding this gentleman and his surname, I recall the maid saying one day that someone had knocked on the door and asked for 'Mister Louse'.[11]

Thus, between work, air raids, and the professional and above all the personal experiences that gradually turned me into an adult, this period that was so traumatic for so many went by. The obliviousness of my youth enabled me to experience the war, at times, as an adventure. Later, down through the years I have come to comprehend all the horror, the suffering and the pain of

---

[11] *Poll* is Catalan for louse.

that time and I wish that there should never be any more wars, anywhere. An utterly utopian wish if we stop to consider what is happening in the world.

At the time, however, not everything was negative: there were also positive things. Cycling eighty kilometres, part of which —as far as Molins de Rei— was a cobbled road, was hard going, but the satisfaction of coming home and putting on the table what you had brought back, knowing that none of the neighbours had half as much, more than compensated for all the effort. This was also the period in my life when I was able to dedicate most time to reading.

I read European authors such as Lajos Zilahy, Axel Munthe and Emil Ludwig, and Catalan novels such as Josep M. de Sagarra's *Vida privada* and Mercè Rodoreda's *Aloma*, which had just won the Creixells prize and had a great impact on me, as did Henry Ford's memoirs, from which I feel sure I learnt a lot. A book of which I have never heard since was *En dono fe*, by the Mallorcan notary Antonio Ruiz Vilaplana, in which he described some of the atrocities committed by the *nacional* side in the repression of the island, which led him to side with the Republic.

III.
Postwar

Marking time

Although this period was not easy, we managed to get by well enough. My father was one of those who did not want to leave when the diaspora took place marked by the entry of the *nacionales* into Barcelona. Staying was not only very dangerous but also meant being unable to work for a long time, never leaving the house and living as discreetly as possible to avoid attracting attention. To amuse himself during this period, he took to writing so as to be doing something that let him feel useful. We lived for many months with the fear that someone would 'squeal' and inform that my father had worked in the Commissariat of Propaganda and had occupied a prominent position there, especially those in the 'guild', who (not all of them, of course!) hurried to report who was who and what they had done.

At that time, as a general rule, it was the concierge who gave 'good' or 'bad' references for the people who lived in their building, and I am convinced that this helped us a lot, because both the concierge at the Commissariat de Propaganda and the one in our building on Carrer del Pi had a high opinion of my father.

After a certain prudential time had passed we were able to return to the world of photography. In those days, application forms were our daily bread. Everything had to be accompanied by the submission of a written application. Especially the manufacturers, who were obliged to fill out an enormous number of forms in order to obtain the various types of certificate and import permit (for machines and a whole range of products…). These documents had to be accompanied by photographs of the place of work, and this allowed us to be photographers again! We dedicated ourselves to the photographic reproduction of this avalanche of paperwork (of course, the photocopier had not yet been invented). Another profitable job at that time, and one that we were obliged to take on, was to photograph paintings by the leading artists, since art exhibitions had become fashionable and there were now galleries of some prestige such as Barcino, Sala Parés, La Pinacoteca and Gaspar —these latter two still exist. The principal buyers of art were manufacturers, especially of fabrics, who even went so far as to acquire entire exhibitions, and the fact is that the fashion for purchasing art was caused by the general state of the market. I shall explain. The government supplied the manufacturers with raw materials at fixed prices and they had to sell their products at prices that were also set by the government. In contrast, in the buying and selling of works of art, the price was freely negotiated. This being so, manufacturing firms would set up a small exhibition room next to the office where they carried out the transactions, and once the invoice had been made out at the legal stipulated prices they took their customers to the adjoining exhibition room and made them buy works of art —by 'a recognised artist'— at whatever price they chose to demand; in this way they mockery of the profit limit set by the government.

Photographs of the dead

I have the feeling that death has never greatly disturbed me, and this being so I accepted, as soon as it was offered to me, a photography job that put me in direct contact with death, with corpses. One evening, just after the war, as we were having supper a gentleman came to the house on the recommendation of a client of my father's. The caller's mother had died, and he wanted a photograph of her. My father did not want to do it, but I readily agreed. I accompanied the gentleman, dressed all in black, to a car of the same hue, which took us to a large house in Sarrià. The dead lady was in one of the rooms, on top of a catafalque. I asked for a stepladder and photographed her from this point of view, from above.

The gentleman then told me how he wanted the photograph and to make this clear showed me a few others that he had hanging in his office. All of them were of deceased family members. I deduced from all of this that in addition to wanting a memento of his relative the man was in fact a collector of photos of the dead. After that first commission there were many others, since this specialism —somewhat macabre, perhaps— enabled me, thanks to the father of the painter Tàpies, to make the acquaintance of the chief forensic pathologist at the Hospital Clínic, Dr Sala Vázquez. When he considered it necessary to have a photograph of one of his cases —a deceased person of particular clinical interest— he would call me, and as I did not suffer from any phobia or neurosis in this regard, I would photograph the body. On one occasion, the Hospital Clínic mortuary kept a dead man in a refrigerator for three days (the time I was away on a trip) until I was available to take his portrait, while the family of the deceased waited.

I also took my first colour photograph at the Hospital Clínic. Dr Sala Vázquez showed me the corpse of a man who had been shot dead in a 'love hotel'. The entry wound was right next to his nose and the bullet hole was very small, surrounded by red spots produced by the bursting of the capillary vessels. The doctor told me that, unfortunately, in a black and white photograph the dots would look like traces of gunpowder. There and then I decided that this would be a colour photograph. I made a trichrome with panchromatic plates, in the same way as practitioners of photogravure do. As I had to make several visits, I made friends with the mortuary attendant who helped me change the posture of the dead man between photographs. He told me that he had worked there during the war, when he was kept busy enough: every morning they would bring him the bodies of those unfortunates who had been taken to the quarry on Montjuïc for a *paseo* in the middle of the night. After shooting them their executioners would go to bed, get up late, have lunch, and in the afternoon come to the Hospital Clínic to view the dead and make comments about what they were like when alive.

The mortuary attendant came to be on friendly terms with the firing squad, and he mentioned to them that the ambulance men who brought the bodies to the hospital used to complain that their job was very hard work, as they had to carry the dead down from the top of the quarry to the ambulance on stretchers, on a very steep path. The firing squad, on the other hand, had it easy, because they took them to be shot when they were still alive, of course, and able to walk up to the top. Having listened to the mortuary attendant, the firing squad agreed that, in order to make things easier, from then on they would do their work down below rather than up at the top of the quarry.

After some time thinking about the fact that families wanted photographs of their dead, I concluded that we all, to a greater or lesser extent, need to preserve the memory of our loved ones. And while this had formerly been in the form of funerary sculpture, writing and painting, the novelty represented by photography as a tool with similar characteristics was also part of the normality of the times. If, in the past, only the well-off could afford to do this, photography has now made available to everyone this means of perpetuating the memory of those they have lost.

Military service

At the end of the war I was 17 years old and a member of the *quinta* or call-up of '43, the first not to be mobilised (the last of those was the 1942 call-up). Following the friendly advice of a friend of my father's, a major, I volunteered, so as to be able to do my compulsory military service, known as the *mili*, in Barcelona itself. However, this meant having to start a year earlier than would have been normal. I was assigned to the Lepanto barracks, in the Signals Regiment of the IV Military District. The barracks was at the far end of Gran Vía, right on the border with L'Hospitalet de Llobregat, an area where there was then still nothing but fields and market gardens. To get there I had to take the metro from Plaça de Catalunya to the Mercat Nou station and continue on foot down Riera Blanca. A walk I have never done since, but one that I would like to do again. In front of the barracks was the *burots* stand, where municipal employees collected the tax on goods entering Barcelona.

After completing the training period and pledging allegiance to the flag, I was assigned to the Optics Section, the section in charge of transmissions and communications. Of course, in those days we had telephones, radio and a carrier pigeon section, but we communicated by morse code, using mirrors during the day and with flashlights at night. I guess they decided to put me there because I was a photographer.

Sometimes when I was on sentry duty at the main gate I would see young men enter the barracks who had done military service during the war but had been mobilised again because of the Second World War. On one of these occasions, I saw a well-built, fair-haired young man whom I already knew: this was the painter Ramon Rogent. Also doing his military service in the same barracks was Tharrats, whom I only met years later, at the weekly *Revista*. On another occasion I saw a horse-drawn carriage arrive to take the chaplain to Montjuïc Castle to attend one of the countless death sentences. However, we never talked about such things. The truth is that despite having lived through the events of the Civil War, we didn't think too much about what was happening. We did whatever we were told to do and that was all. We were young and had a whole lifetime in front of us.

We could leave the barracks only at the weekend, provided we were not on duty. And in fact, because of the World War, we had no idea when our military service would end. Our conscription lasted a longer or shorter period of time —longer for those who had more trouble learning. Every morning and every night, without fail, there was roll call. I still remember the first three names: Panchuelo, Corbacho and Verona. One of the times I was put on kitchen duty, I had to clean a stack of pots and pans that left my hands blacker than coal. When I was finished, I went to the sports ground to try to clean them with sand. The chief cook, who saw me, had a better idea: chop a whole heap of tomatoes to make sauce. Never in my life have my hands been cleaner than they were that day. Another of our regular duties or routines was patrolling the streets. Our itinerary took us

from the barracks to La Rambla. We went in groups of eight or nine
soldiers up and down La Rambla, ensuring that the men who were
off duty did not disturb the peace or cause trouble. This authorised
us to enter brothels or whorehouses, and since we were on duty until
late (two o'clock in the morning), the metro was no longer running,
so we were unable to get back to the barracks to sleep.

Of the officers who commanded us, I recall two in particular:
Captain Cosido, an extremely correct man whom I believe had been
a major, who had been demoted for political reasons. A man who
always looked sad and listless. One year he won the big Christmas
lottery, but his luck was so bad that he got next to nothing, because
he had staked so little. The other officer I remember was Sergeant
Apolinar López Bermejo, a highly disciplined man and the most
energetic in the whole barracks, if somewhat authoritarian.
Nevertheless, I liked him, and I remember that he liked me, too,
because of a chance event one day when I was on the metro from
Plaça de Catalunya to the barracks. At one of the stops, a man came
on with a little boy in his arms, so I politely got up and gave him
my seat, not knowing who he was, of course. When he subsequently
recognised me in the barracks, he always treated me very well, so
much so that, knowing I lived on Carrer del Pi, on the nights when
I was on patrol duty he allowed me to sleep at home.

After I had been doing my military service for just over a year,
I had to go for a medical check-up for the first time because my
teeth hurt. The lieutenant doctor, who was an otolaryngologist,
noticed my nose and subjected me to a whole series of tests. A few
days later he told me that he would fix it for me or, if not, I could
be discharged and go home if he declared me temporarily unfit for
duty. However, he added, there was one drawback: I could never
be either a Civil Guard or a city policeman. Of course, I had no
aspirations to either of these 'trades' and chose to be discharged and
go home, returning to my trade as a photographer.

Out of all that military experience in the period after the
Civil War, I have retained only these few memories. Not as bad as
they might seem with the perspective of the years.

IV.
Working on my own

I become independent of my father
A few years after I finished my military service (which I did a year
earlier than I needed to, in order to stay in Barcelona, in 1942),
I decided to separate from my father —a decision that was hard
and difficult. I realised that if we were not to stagnate and be left
behind, we would have to make some significant changes in the
way we worked. In truth, I did not want a complete break from
my father. I would have liked him to become my partner, but I
was unable to make that happen, and despite the sadness I felt at
having to make such a decision, I was determined to go ahead
with my own professional project. And so I did. I was 25 years old
and the future was mine. Mine alone! The first thing I did was
look for a studio (the same one I still have, on the Travessera de
Dalt). Nevertheless, I continued to live in the family home. My
father was compelled to tell me that I would regret my decision
and I —with all the courage of my 25 years, my eagerness to do
wonderful new things and the confidence I had in myself— replied
that perhaps one day I might come to see that I had been wrong, if
I failed to do what I hoped to, but that I would never, ever regret
having tried.

So I set out to work on my own and on my own account.
But, of course, the only clients I knew were my father's and I
had no intention of taking them. For the time being, then, I
was content to do the jobs that he could not or would not do.
And despite reproaching my decision, he helped me, with a
loan of 5,000 pesetas (which I had to use to lease the studio),

and also gave me bits of equipment that he no longer needed.
I did not have much work to begin with, but I was never idle.
Then the Domecq company announced a very important poster
competition –important above all for the amount of the cash prize:
7,500 pesetas. I decided to enter the competition and submitted
two posters of hand-coloured photographs –not so much (or not
only) for the prize, which was important enough, as for what
it would mean to see them hanging on the wall. And, to my
great surprise, I won. Not long after, I found out that one of the
members of the jury, whose opinion had been decisive in awarding
me the prize, was the director of the Museo del Prado. And one of
his arguments was that he found the image so realistic, as if it were
a photograph; and that decided the jury in my favour. As a result I
was able to repay the loan in just three months.

Slowly but surely, I started to have clients of my own. But
even though the workload was increasing, I still had time to enter
other photography competitions, and I almost always won. One
of these, organised by the Cotolengo del Pare Alegre, was for
photographs of nativity scenes, and the person who presented me
with the prize was the poet Joan Alavedra, who had just returned
from exile. I should say here that the prizes that are most important
to me and have given me greatest satisfaction are the Ciutat de
Barcelona awards. And I say awards –plural– because I have won
these, from my city, on three occasions. Once in 1951, and again
the following year, and for a double win, because I won not
only the photography prize but also the cinema prize with my first
film, *La Ciudad Condal en otoño*. I have gone on to win other prizes,
but these have been given to me by the clients who paid me for
the work I did for them.

The grill room

It was in the fifties, with the launch of the weekly *Revista*, that
I came into contact –close contact– with the world of art and
its leading lights, as I came to know and become good friends
with Tharrats, Guinovart, Cesáreo Rodríguez-Aguilera, Balanyà,

Aleu and a long list of others. Our little circle usually met in the Sala Caralt gallery, in the Tabacos de Filipinas building, on the corner of La Rambla and Carrer del Pintor Fortuny. The first exhibition of the Dau al Set group was held in the Caralt and I had my first exhibition there, which was also the last before the gallery closed for good. Our get-togethers, at which we touched on every kind of subject, were continued over dinner, each day in a different place, but always cheap, as we were all rather short of 'the ready'. We would just as soon go to a little restaurant on Carrer del Bonsuccés as one on Plaça del Pi or on Carrer dels Tallers. We used to prolong our get-together and end up, after dinner, at the Grill Room on Carrer dels Escudellers, a Modernista bar where you could also dance. The music was live, of course, and played by a trio of piano, a saxophone and accordion. It was a kind of blend of jazz and what could be called 'louche' music, because the clientele was very diverse, in every respect. The regulars ranged from the likes of us, artists and intellectuals —'lefties', as they would say now— and people from the port —the workers and, of course, the sailors who came ashore there. It goes without saying that this heterogeneous mix of characters attracted the kind of woman then known as *de mala vida* —living a 'bad life'— whom we called *prosti-puta*,[12] which we thought sounded less harsh or aggressive. The Grill Room was, without a doubt, one of the most curious, most fun places of those years. The pianist, whose name was Miret, was a cultivated man; he had a brother who was a zarzuela singer who had really been quite famous before the war. I remember an amusing anecdote about Miret the pianist. On many nights, a woman would come up close to him while he was playing and whisper something in his ear. When he had finished the number he would lift the lid of the piano and take out a box and hand it to the woman. Of course, this little routine was something of a mystery, until I discovered that the boxes contained the famous nylon stockings that were all the rage among the women. At that time the black market was at its height, and Miret was making some extra money selling stockings!

---

[12]   A portmanteau word combining *prostituta* and *puta* (whore).

However, the roster of curious characters did not start or finish with Miret. There were at least two that I remember who were at least as curious as the pianist. One of these was a man called Joan, who was about sixty, and every time we went to the Grill Room we invariably found him in the same spot, as if he had never left. To such an extent that, jokingly, we used to joke that 'from the bar to the grave'. The other character was a fellow from my neighbourhood, Gràcia, who lived on Sant Josep de la Muntanya. He always took the last tram down to 'town', the 24, at eleven o'clock, and stayed in the place all night until he could catch the first tram back up, at five in the morning.

Most of our group, which consisted of Guinovart, Aleu, Balanyà, Sobregrau, Cesáreo and myself, used to order just coffee there, as we had no money for anything stronger. Only Sobregrau and Cesareo could afford a proper drink. The former was the son of an industrialist and Cesáreo Rodríguez Aguilera was by then a judge in Terrassa. The fact is that, on occasion, some of us didn't even have enough for a coffee, but, naturally, those who were in funds paid for those that were broke.

However, what we mostly did at the Grill Room was observe the scene and enjoy the atmosphere. We hardly ever danced, but since we were young and friendly and a little bohemian, the girls thought of us as pals rather than as potential clients. So much so that they regarded us as friends whom they could trust. On one occasion, when I had an appointment at nine in the morning just off La Rambla, one of the girls invited me to sleep at her place to save me from having to go all the way home and come back down again a few hours later. She didn't charge me a penny, and treated me like a relative, so I slept as if I was all alone and in my own bed at home.

Later, when the American and British 'marines' began to arrive in the port of Barcelona, things began to change. The girls appeared in new dresses and within a couple of months they were all speaking English, or enough, at least, to make themselves understood. In fact, one of the Grill Room girls married an

American sailor —something I discovered quite by chance. One
day, as I was passing the front of the church in Plaça del Pi, I saw a
newly married couple coming out, and to my surprise I recognised
the bride as none other than one of the girls from the Grill Room.
This period was practically the last gasp of that popular bar-cum-
dance hall off La Rambla and of our nights in a place we regarded
as a home from home —somewhere we knew we could take people
to show them a popular hang-out. The fact is that there were many
such unpretentious places, another of which, for our group, was Ca
l'Estevet, where one could eat well for a very good price. It also,
thanks to the art dealer Xifré Morros, gradually became a fantastic
art gallery (as you will see if you go there, even now). Xifré Morros
was one of those who not only believed in but also helped young
artists, especially those who attended the art classes at the Cercle
Artístic. At one point, Xifré Morros proposed a very interesting
arrangement to these young artists that would secure them a few
meals. The idea was that they should each paint a picture of a
certain size, which he would arrange for the restaurant to hang on
its walls and in return give the artist twenty or thirty free meals.
The first restaurant to take part in this unusual eventure was a place
at the Carrer Ample end of Carrer d'Avinyó, and not long after
the same scheme was adopted in Ca l'Estevet, which thus became
a permanent exhibition space. As I have mentioned, this was a
place we frequented, as did old men from the Casa de la Caritat
and employees of the Pompes Fúnebres undertakers, since Estevet
had a set menu at six pesetas and another, a little more substantial,
at eight pesetas. That was at lunchtime, but at night the clientele
was radically different. Then the regulars were, on the one hand,
members of the the artistic fraternity and, on the other, *putes*. The
girls used to sit in a huddle in a back corner, at a table a little larger
than the rest, where as far as I recall could probably accommodate a
dozen or so. A young man called Manolo, who always carried a little
briefcase, sat with them every evening. When the girls had had their
supper, they went back to work in the street, and Manolo came
to join our group and play dominoes. One evening, noticing our

curiosity about his wallet, he showed us what was inside: condoms! This was his small but profitable business, but it was to end quite soon, when Spain, which wished to become part of UNESCO, accepted as a precondition the closure of the houses of prostitution. So it was that the girls and Manolo found themselves out of work and the back table was left empty, but only for a short time, because our group quickly occupied it. In the end, Manolo stayed on at Ca l'Estevet as a waiter.

As for some of the characters I had the good fortune to meet and photograph, in addition to those I have already mentioned there was La Chunga, whom I came to know by way of Paco Revés and our get-togethers at the Sala Caralt gallery. One day Revés showed up with a little Roma girl who must have been about twelve years old and who posed for him as a model. She also danced flamenco –and very well, I must add. Now, Paco Revés was a very well-connected young man who used to go to so-called 'society' parties, and he often took the Roma girl to dance at them. On those occasions when our gang tagged along to one of these parties, we would pass a hat around for the other guests to throw in some money for the girl and her people –an old man called Ramon, who played the guitar, and a young boy who danced.

La Chunga lived in the Roma neighbourhood of Montjuïc –very close to where the Miró Foundation is now– which was one of the many shanty towns at that time. She and I had become friends, and she would occasionally say to me: 'Are you coming to *la ropa* on Sunday?' In saying *la ropa* –'clothes'– she meant her house, since the Roma tended not to have a fixed abode but a place where they kept their clothes. In due course she became one of the regulars at our suppers at Ca la Mariona, when she was already a professional *bailaora* or flamenco dancer.

When La Chunga started dancing professionally she had to join the union, and when she went to register she took her mother. When they asked La Chunga for her full name, she answered: 'Micaela Flores Amaya.' And when she was asked where she was born she said 'In a bean field', outside a little town in the south of

France where Roma people gathered every year. They were unable to give the exact date or time of her birth, the only clue that her mother could offer was that 'the little beans were so small'.

On one of her tours of the United States, while staying in a hotel in New York, the *maître* complained to Revés that Ramon was shitting behind the curtains that lined the lounge corridors. Paco naturally asked Ramon why he didn't use the toilets like everyone else, and Ramon replied that they disgusted him. Frankly, I understood him, since Ramon had always lived like a Roma, in the open air, but the rest of our gang started to call him the Human Fly, because he used to shit everywhere, as flies do. La Chunga's father worked as a hod carrier, and when she became a professional flamenco dancer and was earning more than enough to support the family, he kept on working, although now he went to work in a taxi. Some time later, when La Chunga had plenty of money, she told her family that she wanted to buy them a flat, but they said no, and in the end she bought them a walled plot in Santa Coloma de Gramenet where they could live just as they had in the shack o Montjuïc, but now feeling they were Roma aristocracy.

La Chunga only learned to read and write when she was an adult. She drew very well, with a certain naïve style, and I still have a Christmas card that she made for me. I also have a photograph I took of her with Miró –to whom I introduced her– in a flamenco place on Carrer dels Escudellers. Miró is sitting with La Chunga and Valerie, an English friend of mine. The photo, by the way, reminds me of *La verbena de la Paloma* –'The Fair of the Virgin of La Paloma'– because of 'a brunette and a blonde'.

Sí senyor

In the sixties I started working for a special client, and continued to do so for a good number of years. I really enjoyed the work, not only because I liked photographing the objects he created, but also because we shared a commitment to devoting ourselves to our respective trades with great enthusiasm and dedication. I would like to put together a book of the many photos of his pieces I have in my archive, to show how very advanced he was in his field, which was that of a decorator and furniture maker. He had a large workshop in Les Corts, and a big shop on the Diagonal, and his name was Ramon Carrera.

He designed the interiors of a lot of restaurants, some of which received a great deal of attention, and because he really threw himself into his work, he came to understand more about restaurants than the restaurateurs themselves. A proof of this is that he was the first to create a gas kitchen in Barcelona, despite the misgivings of the chef.

In 1982, Ramon had the idea of converting his shop on Carrer de Mallorca, which had formerly been a real dairy with cows until the City Council banned the custom, to open a restaurant of his own, exactly to his taste. He called the place Sí Senyor —'yes sir'. From time to time he would host a special lunch there for friends and business associates, and this soon became a regular Wednesday fixture —a day off to get together and chew the fat as we used to do. For more than ten years now we have been meeting there every Wednesday to eat, talk, listen, disagree, and have a great time. Before then, Sunday was my weekly day of rest, but now, thanks to these get-togethers, Wednesday is my holiday and I hope it will continue to be so for many years to come.

Group photos

The idea of the team or group shapes the social reality through which one thinks of achieving some purpose. In Romanesque mural painting we already find this concept of a group centred on a figure, the Christ Pantocrator, who is almost always depicted with the twelve apostles and the four evangelists grouped around him, and sculpted capitals also usually feature groups of biblical characters or animals. Naturally, photography —the modern representation of people and groups— has also done this and still does. We portray or photograph families, football and basketball teams, demonstrations, theatre groups and music groups, etcetera. And I have done this myself, many, many times. One of the

occasions I recall most fondly was with the so-called Grup de
Taüll, a group of visual artists that was formed on the occasion of
the Biennal Hispanoamericana d'Art held in Barcelona in 1955
or 1956, I don't remember which. The group was formed in the
hope that some of the prizes that to be were awarded might stay
in Catalonia, and the photo was taken at the Museu d'Art de
Catalunya, which houses the most famous and most marvellous
Pantocrator, from Taüll, which is precisely what gave the group
its name. Once the photo was taken, the group disbanded, but its
members were Tàpies, Cuixart, Muxart, Tharrats, Aleu, Guinovart
and Jordi Mercader, seven young and subsequently outstanding
exponents of Catalan contemporary art.

Another group photo that I had the privilege of taking, rather
more recently, was for the Spanish television programme *Los años
vividos*, which brought together various people from a given
decade and a photographer of the same generation to immortalise
the group. I chose to take the photo of my generation (born
in the 1920s) in the Parque del Retiro in Madrid, on the steps
overlooking the lake; this allowed me a diagonal view of the group,
making the shot more dynamic. There were almost thirty of us,
including such notable personalities as Fraga Iribarne, Sara Montiel,
Nicolás Redondo, Berlanga and others. Of course, these were not
the only group portraits I took: I also photographed groups of less
well-known but no less important people —factory workers, those
figures on the capitals of various churches…

The fact is that from a technical perspective (there are
not too many secrets to taking a group photo), for this type of
photography the most important thing is collaboration; next, that
the light should come from above, from a single source, and it
should be natural. The people do not need to strike a pose or adopt
any special attitude, they just need to position themselves just as
they are, in their own way, as they feel most comfortable, because
otherwise it would be an act and I always prefer people to be
themselves, their true selves, because I am particularly averse to
manipulating the image of people to make them look good.

V.
Characters

Albert Puig Palau

In the fifties there was a feeling that something might be about
to change in Spain. It had been more than ten years since the
imposition of General Franco's dictatorship and a significant number
of people, some of whom had been linked to Franco and the Falange
until then, were starting to try to bring about political change in
Spain. One of these was Dionisio Ridruejo, a renegade Falangist.

Here in Catalonia a group of writers –Eugeni d'Ors, Carles
Riba, J. M. Sagarra and Rossend Llates– decided to launch a new
weekly magazine, to be called *Revista*, with the financial backing
of that curious character Albert Puig Palau. I had already done
a couple of photo-essays for the weekly magazine *Destino*, and I
was introduced to the group behind the new weekly by Llates,
who was a very good friend of my father. Puig Palau was a textiles
manufacturer who had been with the *nacionales*, where he held the
rank of lieutenant. He could be described as a vulgar snob, but it
is worth bearing in mind that his connection with the 'winners'
facilitated the publication of the magazine, through which he
helped to promote many young artists of the time who, thanks
to *Revista*, were able to publish and make their work known. Of
these, special mention should be made of Guinovart, Tharrats and
myself. Joan Prats used to say that snobs were a necessary type
because, thanks to their need to show off and be noticed, they were
disposed to help promote little-known young artists. And, in effect,
in those years *Revista* was an important tool for drawing attention
to the work of young artists, journalists and intellectuals. The

articles that Rodríguez-Aguilera wrote each week about one of
these new artists were illustrated with a photograph by me.

Thanks, too, to Puig Palau's intellectual pretentions, he
invited Cocteau, Foujita, the composer Georges Auric and other
famous people to his estate by the Castell beach in Palamós, and
we would also go there to discuss *Revista* business and at the same
time to meet this procession of celebrity guests. It was during his
stay at Puig Palau's place that Georges Auric composed the music
for the film *Moulin Rouge*, about the painter Toulouse-Lautrec,
starring the actor José Ferrer. In fact, the main theme was inspired
by a Catalan popular song which, if my memory serves me, is 'La
Filadora'. Many years later, on the occasion of a Miró exhibition at
the Grand Palais in Paris, I went to the artist's house to photograph
him. This was at the time of the execution of Puig Antich and the
formal opening of the exhibition became an act of homage to Puig
Antich. I remember that Ibáñez Escofet, Raimon, Tàpies were also
there, and Tàpies painted a mural…

I must admit that during the three years of *Revista*'s existence
—whose contributors, in addition to the aforementioned, also
included Aleu, Sordo and Molist— we had a great time. We used
to have our editorial meetings at the Hotel Ritz, especially when
Dalí was in town on his way to or from America, since it was he
who had designed and drawn the magazine's header. As I said,
the magazine only lasted three years, but during that time we
kept up the hope of political change in Spain. Needless to say, the
disappointment was severe! I was to become acquainted with all the
members of the Dau al Set group after it was founded, in 1947, and
although we were not close friends I got on well with all of them.

Ponç, for example, went to Brazil and I rarely heard anything
from him except for one occasion, when he was in Cadaqués and
called to ask me to come and take some photos of him. I drove up
in my SEAT 600, accompanied by Joanet Artigas and his Japanese
wife Mako. Oddly enough, when we arrived at his house we
found he was out. In fact he was waiting for us at the Casino and
although he had seen me go past, when he saw me with a Japanese

woman he took me for Japanese. Despite the misunderstanding we did meet in the end and I took the photos he wanted. I met Josep Pla at *Destino* and went on to illustrate some of his books. I even went to his farmhouse in Llofriu on one occasion, but we didn't quite hit it off, though I don't really know why. He wrote the book, I was given the finished texts, I took the photographs and that was that.

By the time I met Sebastià Gasch he was already an important man. I had heard about him from my father and of course I knew about the famous *Manifest Groc*. We met during the Grill Room period, and it was our group who introduced him to La Chunga, in a tavern in Sarrià. It was really Gasch who promoted La Chunga. I must thank him, however, for referring to my photographs in very flattering terms in a couple of articles in *Destino*. When I met Gasch, I was quite shocked by the fact that this important critic, a major figure in the intellectual and journalistic life of Barcelona, could not live on what he earned by his writing but had to stuff envelopes and run errands for Vinçon.

I worked with Carles Sentís for a while, doing photojournalism for Scandinavia. In one of these we did an interview with Alfonso de Borbón, the king's cousin, who at that time was the Spanish ambassador to Sweden. On one occasion with Sentís I happened to mention a series of articles about migrants from Murcia who came to Catalonia on a train that the author of the articles dubbed Transmiscria, and he told me he had written those articles —what a coincidence! As a matter of fact, a compilation of these articles has recently been published. I became friends with his whole family, and in fact I already knew his sister Maria Dolors: some years before, she and Guinovart and I, with a few others, had tried to set up an advertising agency that never really came to anything.

Picasso

I would love to have met Picasso in person, and in fact on several occasions there seemed to be a chance I might do so. Needless to say, I was captivated by the idea of photographing him, but the connection between us was always indirect.

My first contact with Picasso was by way of Xavier Busquets, the architect of the new Col·legi d'Arquitectes building on Plaça Nova. Through Cinto Raventós, a great friend of the painter, Busquets arranged to visit Picasso in France to ask if he would design a large mural or frieze, to be made in ceramics, for the façade of the Col·legi. Picasso was keen on the idea, but said that the mural should be made not with ceramic tiles but with a new process developed by the Norwegian Carl Nesjar for creating reliefs on concrete walls using high-pressure sandblasting to strip away the concrete and expose a substrate of black pebbles. The resulting *sgraffito* was surprising for the similarity obtained from the comparison with the graphics obtained by plastering a rough wall. The line obtained in this way is never uniform but broken, as the contrast between the black pebbles and the white concrete reproduced it perfectly.

Busquets then travelled to Oslo to ask Carl Nesjar if he would carry out the work. Of course he accepted the commission with enthusiasm, saying that it would be a great pleasure to visit Barcelona again, adding that he had two friends in the city: Marc Aleu and Català-Roca. Carl, a versatile artist who was also keenly interested in photography, had previously spent some time in Barcelona and Cadaqués with his wife, who was a painter.

After another trip to the south of France to see Picasso, Busquets brought the original drawings for me to reproduce. Carl came to Barcelona to do the murals, and I set to photographing the drawings and making enlarged prints, which had to be the same size as the finished murals, as I shall now explain. During the sandblasting process, Carl needed to protect his eyes from abrasion by wearing goggles, the lenses of which had to be replaced frequently as exposure to the sandblasting and the fine particles of concrete led to a loss of visibility. This impaired visibility called for a tremendous effort of concentration, both mental and physical, going over a full-scale photographic enlargement in the hotel room, time after time, to memorise the lines he would execute the next day almost from memory, with the considerable additional responsibility of having to recreate nothing less than the outline of a genuine Picasso.

When the work was finished, I remember reading a newspaper article which disparaged the frieze for looking like scribbles made by a child, when that was precisely the intention; the author of the article had entirely failed to appreciate the mural as yet another manifestation of Picasso's genius and his love of the city in which he had spent a crucial part of his youth. I believe that, although muted, this disdainful attitude persists, and yet we surely have the greatest Picasso in the world, a work he conceived with a perfect knowledge of the dimensions and technical characteristics of the commission, but paradoxically very little attention is paid to it. At the same time no one hesitates to attribute La Pedrera to Antoni Gaudí, even though he probably never laid a single tile there.

Picasso's exceptional level of visual perception and retention is clearly apparent in a beautiful anecdote related to a poster I did for the Ministry of Information and Tourism, which reproduced a detail of a Romanesque painting, specifically an eye and part of the face of the Taüll Pantocrator. The poster was in colour, and I made a life-size mock-up in black and white which I sent to Madrid along with the slide. The project had stalled, but then Fraga was appointed minister and when he saw the mock-up he said: 'This poster —let it be made.' I also seem to recall that the thing won a major international award. Now, Busquets gave one of these posters to Picasso, who immediately asked him which Pantocrator it was. 'The one from Taüll,' Busquets replied. 'No, it can't be the Taüll.' 'Yes, that's what Català-Roca told me.' To settle the dispute, Picasso fetched a book that had a reproduction of the same Pantocrator and, comparing the two images, pronounced: 'Right to left.' And he was absolutely right, because when I was studying a slide of the painting in the viewer to select a suitable framing, I realised that I much preferred the way it looked when it was reversed. No doubt due to the Western habit of reading from left to right, the resulting image was more striking, which is precisely one of the qualities I most appreciate in a poster. In the mid 'eighties, the Musée Picasso in Paris called to tell me that they had found in the artist's studio a dozen photos of bullfights that I had taken in Spain in the fifties, and asked if they could use them. I said yes, with great pleasure, and it made me very happy to think that my beloved photos of bulls had had such an important admirer.

Now we must talk about *Guernica*. I had always been intrigued by the fact that the most important painter of the twentieth century had made this monochrome painting, without colour, and I deduced that what he wanted to represent was war. But Picasso had never been in a war, so any visual knowledge he had of it was from photographs and films and therefore always in black and white. In fact, the first sketches for *Guernica* are in colour, and I have a feeling that the photographer Dora Maar, who was Picasso's companion at the time, took monochrome shots of these, and when he saw them he understood that the absence of colour made for a documentary reading that added a testimonial value to the pathos, evoking the same emotions that he felt on receiving news of the war. And the 'document' that is *Guernica* will possibly be seen as the most emblematic work of art of the twentieth century. This theory about Picasso's use of monochrome would be confirmed by the 1944 painting *Ossuary*, about the concentration camps, where the absence of colour again creates a parallel with the only visual references Picasso would have had on the subject, namely photographs and documentary footage. On the other hand, the contemporaneous painting *Night Fishing in Antibes* is in colour, as he had taken the scene from nature.

Returning to the *sgraffiti* of the Col·legi d'Arquitectes, allow me tell an anecdote related to Miró. One day I mentioned to Busquets that I was going to Mallorca the following day to see Miró, and he said to me: 'Well, ask him for me if he would do something for us for the Col·legi d'Arquitectes.' I did so the next evening, when, after working all day, we were having dinner in a very popular restaurant in Inca: Miró was happy and in very good humour, but when I mentioned Busquets' request he became very serious and asked me: 'And what do they want me to do for them? The toilets?' I did not labour the point, and I subsequently learned that the initial idea had been for Picasso to do the three friezes on the façade, while Miró would have the two walls inside the building next to the assembly hall, where the 'Arches' wall and the 'Sardana' wall, both by Picasso, are now. What happened is that when Busquets went to collect the originals of the three 'Mediterranean' friezes, Picasso also gave him two more original sketches, intended for the walls supposedly asigned to Miró. Busquets reminded Picasso of this, and the latter replied: 'I'll do them for you, the Mirós.' And, picking up a piece of charcoal, he added eyes, crosses and spots to the drawing of the sardana.

Miró never forgot this, and I believe it is the reason why, a few years later, when a group of young architects invited him to hold an exhibition at the Col·legi, he accepted. He always sided with the young, and he duly painted the plate glass windows of the Col·legi, but he stipulated that at the end of the exhibition the paintings were to be washed off, in order to ensure that no one could make a profit from them.

Miró

The truth is that my first acquaintance with Miró was when I was just ten or eleven years old, because my father often spoke to us about him, as he had taken several photographs of hats from the shop owned by Joan Prats, a close friend of Miró's. In other words, I grew up knowing Miró's name, but I did not know him personally until the fifties, when Thomas Bouchard came to Barcelona to make a documentary film about him. I was Bouchard's photographer and my relationship with Miró became closer with each day that passed, since I was spending a lot of time in his studio in order to capture him in his actual working environment. The fact is that at first it was not easy, since Miró – shy by nature– did not really like being watched as he worked. The early stage of my involvement in his work was a little difficult, then, but as I was not much given to talking either —nor am I now, when I work— we soon came to understood one another. He worked and I took photos. In this way, by being a kind of shadow, I entered on a professional relationship with Miró that lasted thirty years! It's easy to say, isn't it?

One of the things we had in common was a concern for punctuality. On one occasion we hwere to travel to Palautordera together for some work he was going to do there, so we arranged that I should pick him up each day during the week that he was to go there, at ten in the morning. I would arrive ten minutes early in my SEAT 600 (by then I had replaced the Vespa with a car); he would wait for me in front of his hotel reading the newspaper and when the church bell struck ten he would walk into the foyer; there Miró was already waiting for me there, who, like me, also headed to the lobby as soon as he heard the chimes. And that was not the only thing that brought me together with Miró; one of the others was the fact that he always got along very well with his assistants and the people he worked with, whose suggestions and initiatives he actually welcomed. He was even happy to be surprised.

Some of his truest helpers and collaborators were his almost worn-out old brushes, which he jealously guarded and continued to use for as long as possible, because with them the line was not uniform but broken and irregular.

Of course, I always tried to take my photographs without him noticing, which is why, in many of these shots, the painter has his back to me. One of the photo series that I recall with particular pleasure was taken as Miró —with his back to me— was looking at the three paintings he made in tribute to Salvador Puig Antich and which he titled *The Hope of a Condemned Man*. In these photos, Miró's head is in front of the bare bulb that lit the room and made an arc of light appear around it. With this photo, I wanted to perpetuate a joke that a friend of his had made years before, saying to him they could see a halo around his head: Miró thought that his hair was messed up and immediately put his hands to his head before realising it was a joke. However, on a few occasions I managed to take a photo of his face, but I could only allow myself to do so at times when he was so intensely absorbed in his work that he did not even see me; some of the shots in which Miró is seen with an expression of suffering or satisfaction are from such moments.

Although we did not speak much, my relationship with Miró was always very close, so much so that I accompanied him almost everywhere. He had a big retrospective exhibition at the Museo de Arte Contemporáneo in Madrid, which was inaugurated by the king and queen, of old works, that is, many years old and that had been loaned by museums and private collectors from all over the world. After making the official tour of the exhibition, Miró said that he would like to see it again in a calmer fashion –if possible, without anyone else– and the museum director suggested that he come back the following Monday. I was based in Madrid at the time, and we agreed that I would pick him up at the airport on the Monday for the private visit. We had lunch at the Palace Hotel and then Miró went up to his room for a siesta, as was his habit. In the meantime, I went ahead to the museum so that everything would be ready to receive him. When Miró arrived, they took him straight up in the goods lift, without even getting out of the taxi, and hand in hand, because he was already quite advanced in years, we made the tour together. He looked at the paintings very attentively, then suddenly stopped and, turning to me, said: 'This young fellow will go far!' He had a self-deprecating sense of humour. That afternoon, Miró had a great time. Someone who didn't have such a great time was the taxi driver, who thought, when they made him drive into the lift, that it was a kidnapping. They even had to give him a brandy to settle his nerves!

I have already said that Miró and I tended not to talk much, since we were both intensely dedicated to our work. But of course, on some occasions we would have a chat, even if it was just a little. On one of these occasions, Miró told me that Picasso would be the greatest painter of the twentieth century and immediately

added that he himself would be the greatest painter of the twenty-
first. And in my opinion, he was not wrong. However, he did not
usually talk about other painters. On one occasion when I told
him that I was going to see a Chagall exhibition, he said to me:
'Chagall…?' in a somewhat derogatory tone, from which I deduced
that he did not like Chagall's work or that they were not on good
terms. Nevertheless, although he gave the impression of being a
rather quiet, serious character, the fact is that when Artigas or I
told him a joke or a funny story he was always happy to share a
moment of joy and laughter. At the same time, he placed a great
deal of trust in me, because I never asked questions. If he wanted
to tell me something, I always listened to him, and always very
attentively. And whenever he asked me for my opinion I would
give it to him very sincerely. On the many occasions that we
went somewhere together in my car, he would sit next to me and
take notes. He always carried some paper or a little notepad and
something to write with. Happily, I still have some of those notes
that Miró made in his small and sometimes illegible handwriting.
He used to attend get-togethers with the surrealists, but as a rule
he would simply listen. I am convinced that of all that group of
artists, the one who got the most out of those gatherings was
Miró, precisely because he used to listen and reflect. Although he
used to go there and frequent them, he was not their close friend;
without a doubt, his great friend was Josep Llorens i Artigas, who,
ahead of an exhibition in Paris of ceramics by this extraordinary
Miró–Artigas tandem, asked me to take some photos of the pieces
before they were sent off. From then on I worked with them on
a regular basis, in a collaboration that, as I have said, was to last for
thirty years. Thirty years in which what all three of us were most
interested in was working, working… We were clear that only
thorough, serious, painstaking work can produce real quality. And
that is what we dedicated ourselves to.

Of note among Miró's other collaborators was the director of
the Maeght gallery in Barcelona, Paco Farreras, and his wife Núria,
who were instrumental in Miró receiving commissions for public

artworks in Barcelona, such as the mural at the airport, the Pla de l'Ós mosaic on the pavement of La Rambla, or the monumental sculpture *Woman and Bird* in the park on the former site of the municipal slaughterhouse, now named Parc de Joan Miró. Very close by, where Carrer de Llançà meets Gran Via, there is building crowned with a large Modernista butterfly, which served as inspiration both being *trencadís* broken tile mosaics. I believe that in time *Woman and Bird* will become the great emblematic symbol of Barcelona, replacing the Columbus monument: the latter represented the achromatic era very well, but we are now living in the age of colour.

Llorens Artigas

When I was Bouchard's assistant, I had to accompany him to Gallifa, the town where the ceramist Llorens Artigas had his house and studio. The farmhouse was called El Racó and it was where they were both working on the pieces that were to form the Paris exhibition entitled *Terres de Grand Feu* –'earths of great fire'. That was the start of my collaboration with these two exceptional artists who were to be so important (though I could hardly have suspected it at the time) for my life and, especially, for my work.

Gallifa was and is one of the smallest towns in Catalonia, and of course in those days it had neither electricity nor a telephone line. To get there we had to take a bus to Sant Feliu de Codines, from where the only taxi would take us on to Gallifa and El Racó. By the way, on one of these trips in the taxi, the taxi driver turned to me and said: 'I don't know this gentleman you're going to see, nor do I know exactly what he does, but from what I hear, he's up there with Kubala.' What a footballing compliment![13]

Artigas was married to a Swiss lady named Violette, who was known as 'Senyora Madame' by the locals. She was actually a very nice woman, a lovely lady in a few words and an excellent cook. I think she held me in high esteem, because I was properly

[13] László Kubala was a Hungarian footballer who played for FC Barcelona in the 1950s, scoring 131 goals.

appreciative of her cooking. In this respect I was the opposite of
Brossa. On one occasion when he was invited to El Racó, Violette
had gone to considerable trouble to prepare an exquisite dish (a
suckling pig) and Brossa could think of nothing better than to ask
for a fried egg.

Artigas would sometimes sign a work with a diminutive of
his surname, ARTI, and if anyone asked him why, he would answer
that he signed ARTI to save on GAS.

I am convinced —and leading scholars share this opinion— that
Artigas was a real innovator in the art of ceramics, although he
very definitely did not like to use the electric kiln. He claimed that
pieces fired in it always came out uniform, all the same, whereas
with the wood-fired kiln, each piece was unique. This is precisely
what Miró was looking for when he decided to work the field of
ceramics, and the basis of why they got along so well. Miró and
Artigas turned defects into quality and perfection. On one occasion
when Artigas broke a piece that he considered had not come out
well enough, Miró carefully picked up all the fragments and later
used them on a sculpture. They really did constitute a spectacular
trio —and I say trio, because in addition to the two of them the
necessary third element was fire. I am in no doubt that it was
Artigas' contribution that made Miró an exceptional ceramist. Miró
was a serious man by nature, while Artigas, who was very serious
in his work and in his art, was at the same time a very pleasant,
affable fellow. Once, when Miró gave him a painting as a gift, he
naturally hung it in a prominent place in his house, and when an
art dealer who frequently visited him noticed this Miró, he offered
to buy it. Artigas said no, of course, because it had been a gift from
his friend, but when Miró found out —knowing as he did that
Artigas was still paying off the mortgage on his house— he told
him to sell it without a second thought. In due course the dealer
paid another visit, he offered him a very high price. Artigas used
to laugh and say how lucky it was that he was leaning against the
wall at that moment, because otherwise he would have fallen over
backwards when he heard the sum the dealer offered him. In fact,

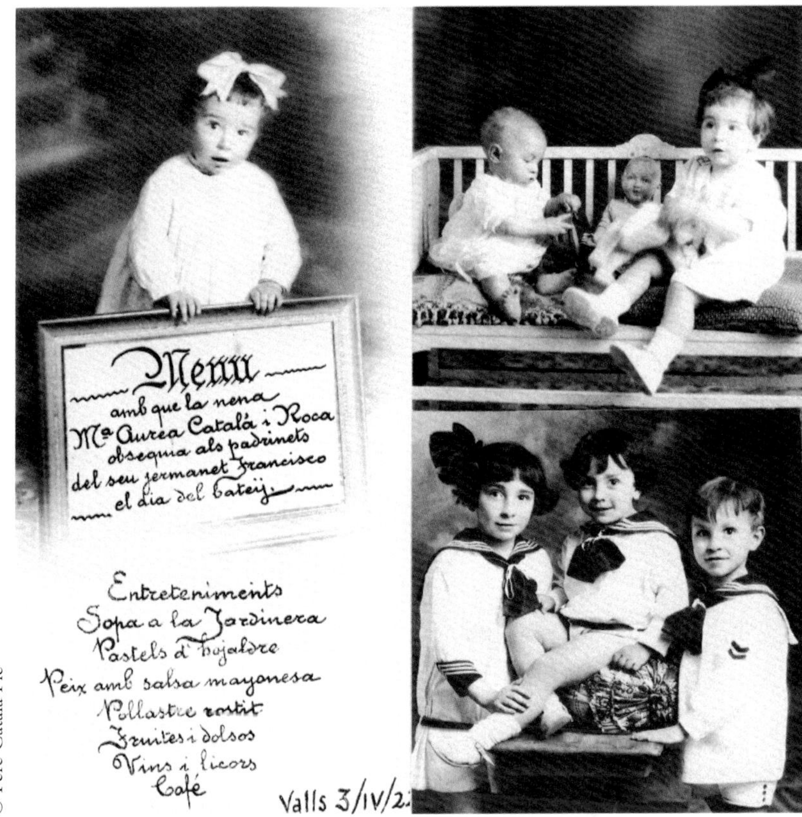

Invitation for the lunch on the occasion of my baptism, which took place the day after my name day; therefore, I had to wait a whole year to celebrate it.

With my older sister. The three siblings dressed as 'sailors,' as it was called in those days.

The composition and layout of the images is original, created by Francesc Català-Roca.

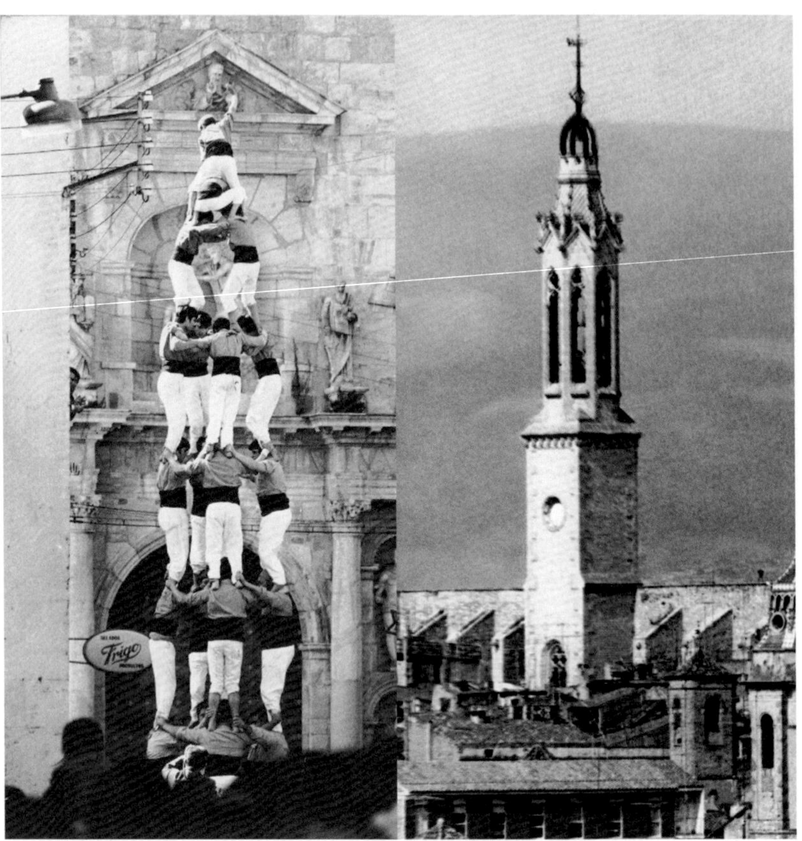

Two images of Valls, my hometown. The Castell "quatre de vuit" and the bell tower of Sant Joan church—I find they have great similarities.

On the next page:
End-of-year group at Comtal School.
Standing guard at the gate of the Lepanto barracks.
Portrait from when I became independent.
Giving my son Martí his first photography lesson.
Martí and Andreu helping me set up an exhibition.
With my grandson Mark, who, if he wishes, c
ould be the fourth generation of photographers.

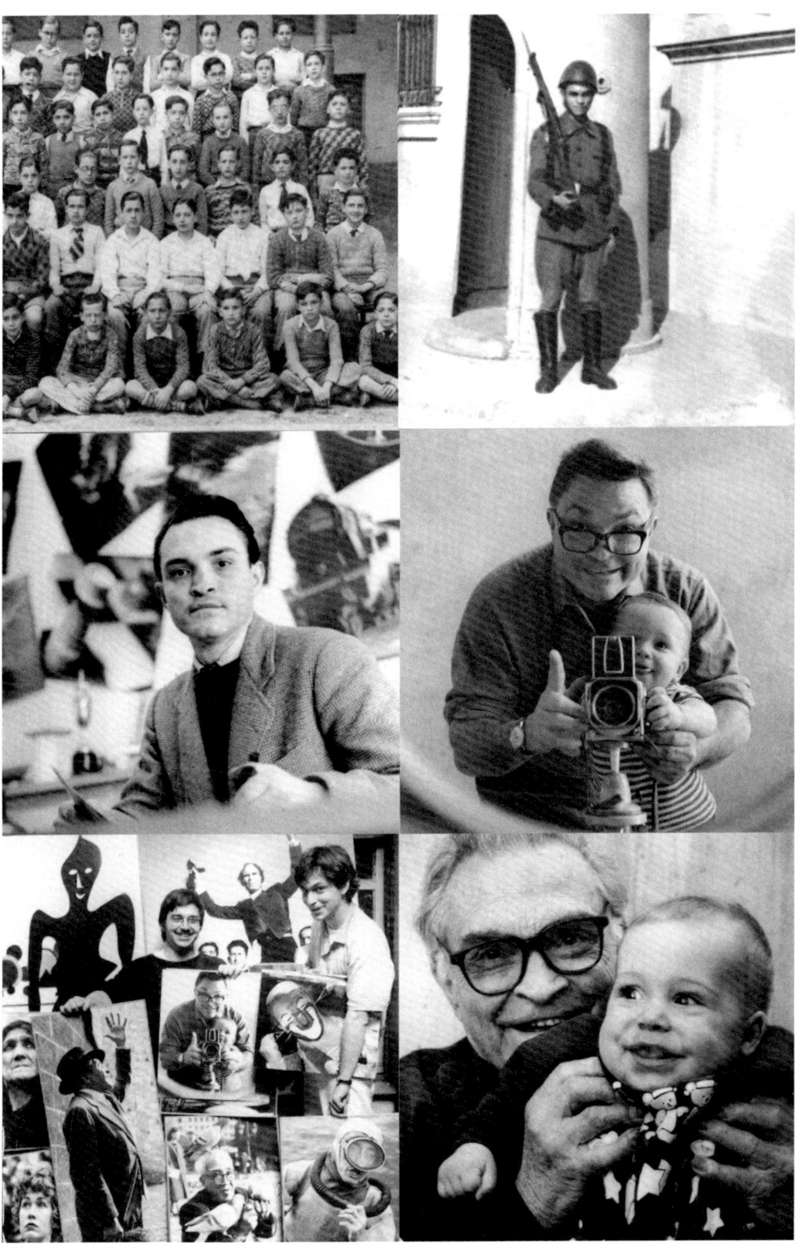

Original photo in colour

© Andreu Català Pedersen / Original photo in colour

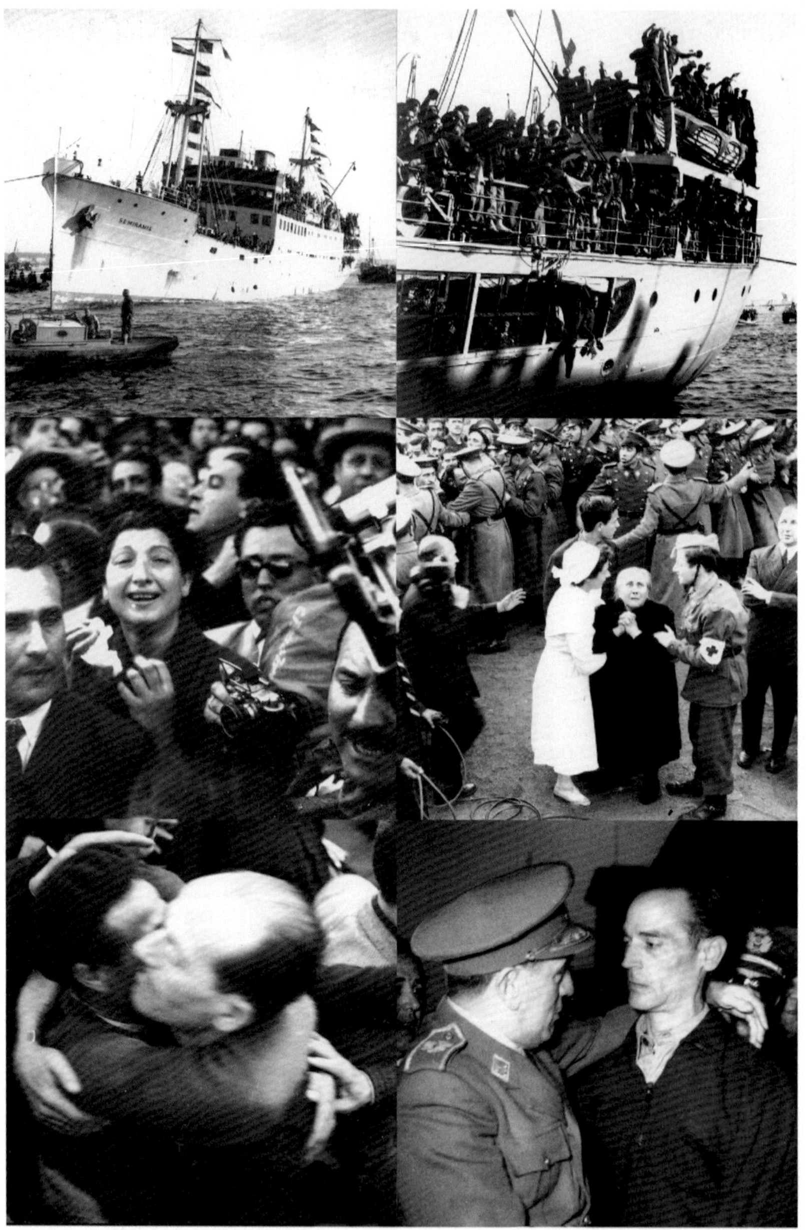

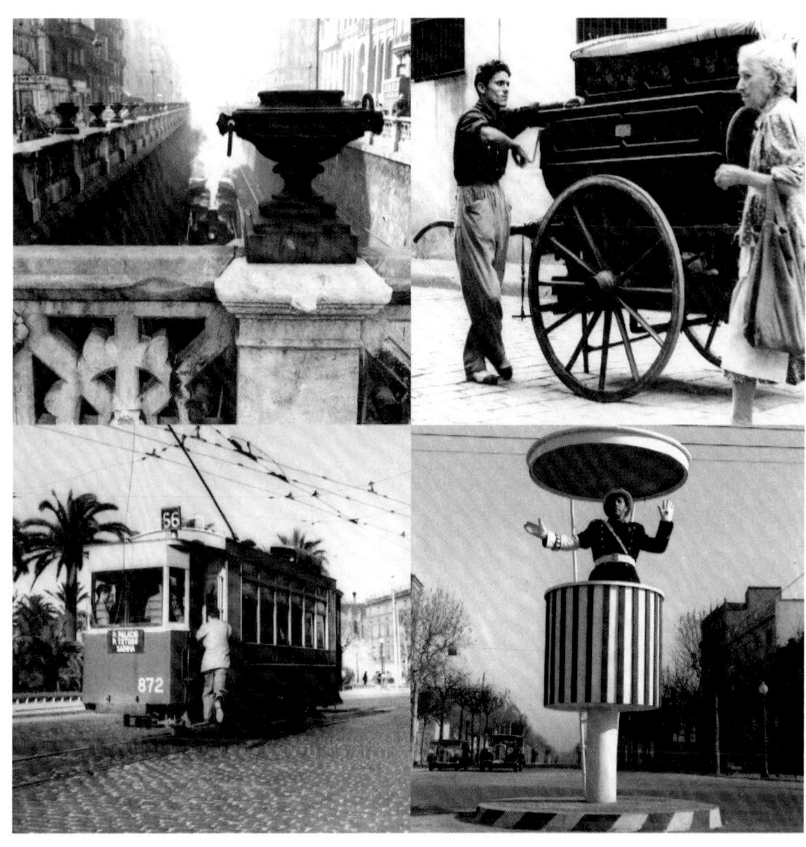

Things from Barcelona that have already disappeared.

On the previous page:
Report on the arrival at the port of Barcelona of the ship Semiramis,
which was bringing back the ex-prisoners of the Blue Division.

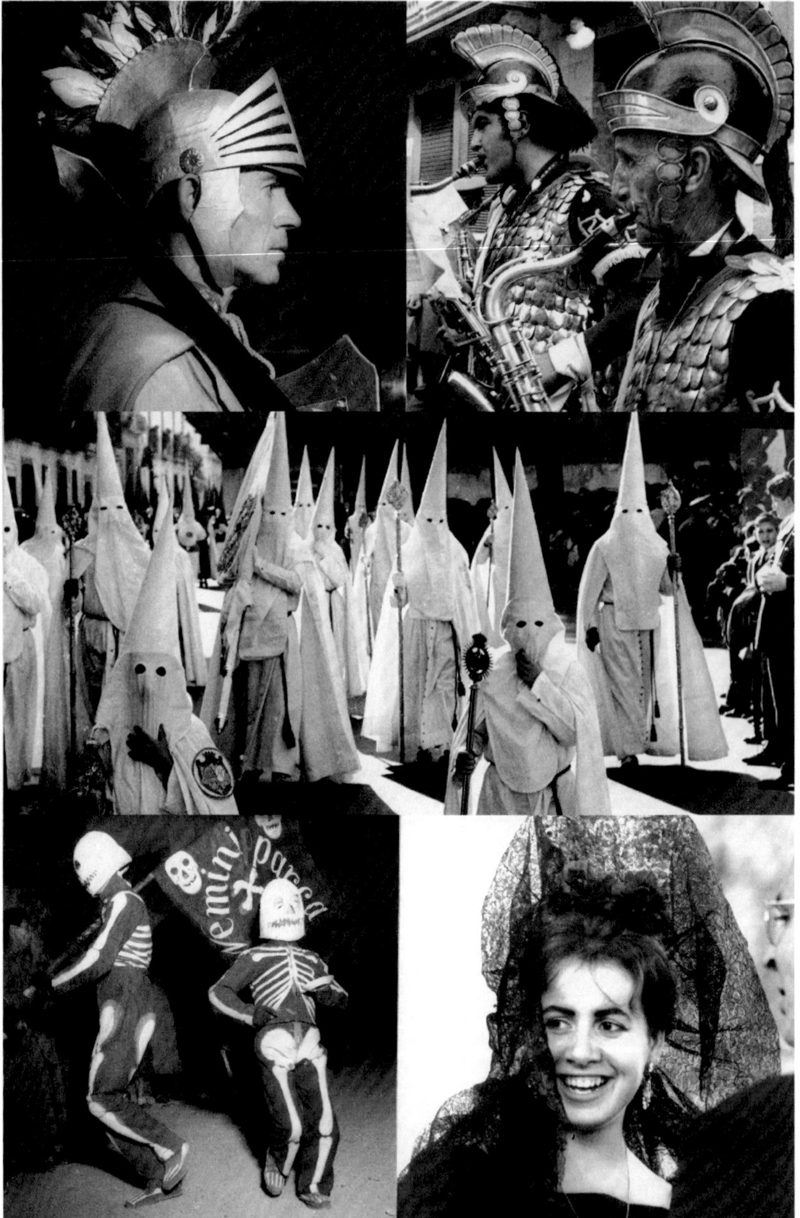

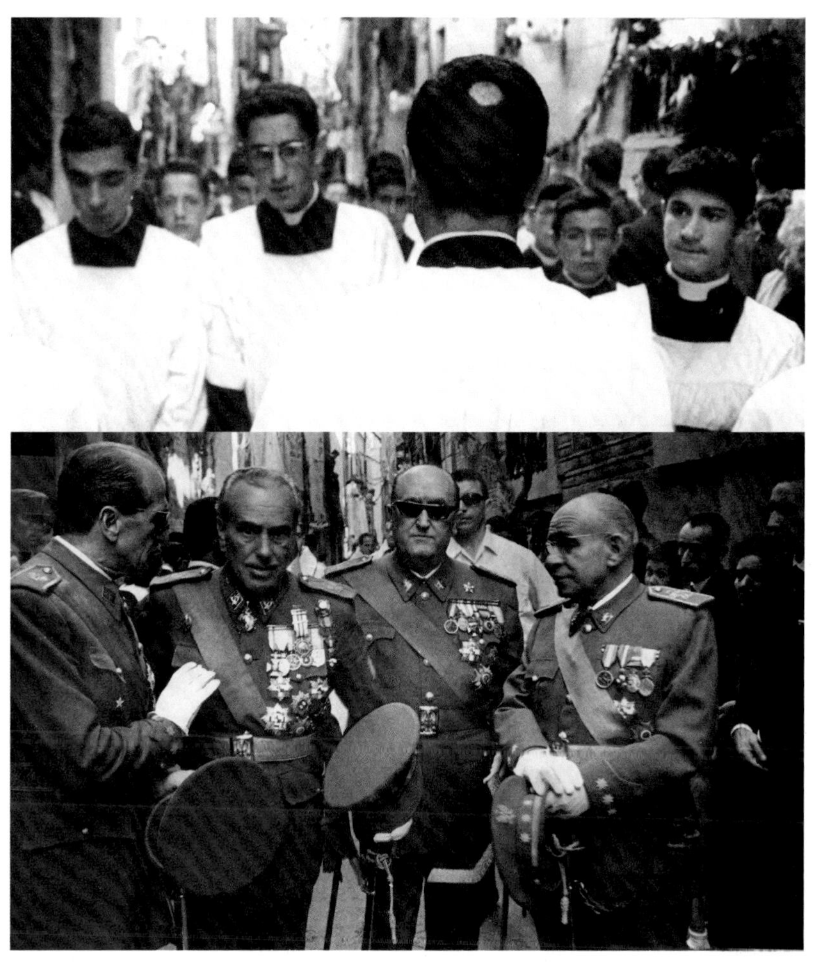

Corpus Christi celebration in Toledo, with priests and soldiers.

On the previous page:
Holy Week processions in Verges, Lorca, and Seville.

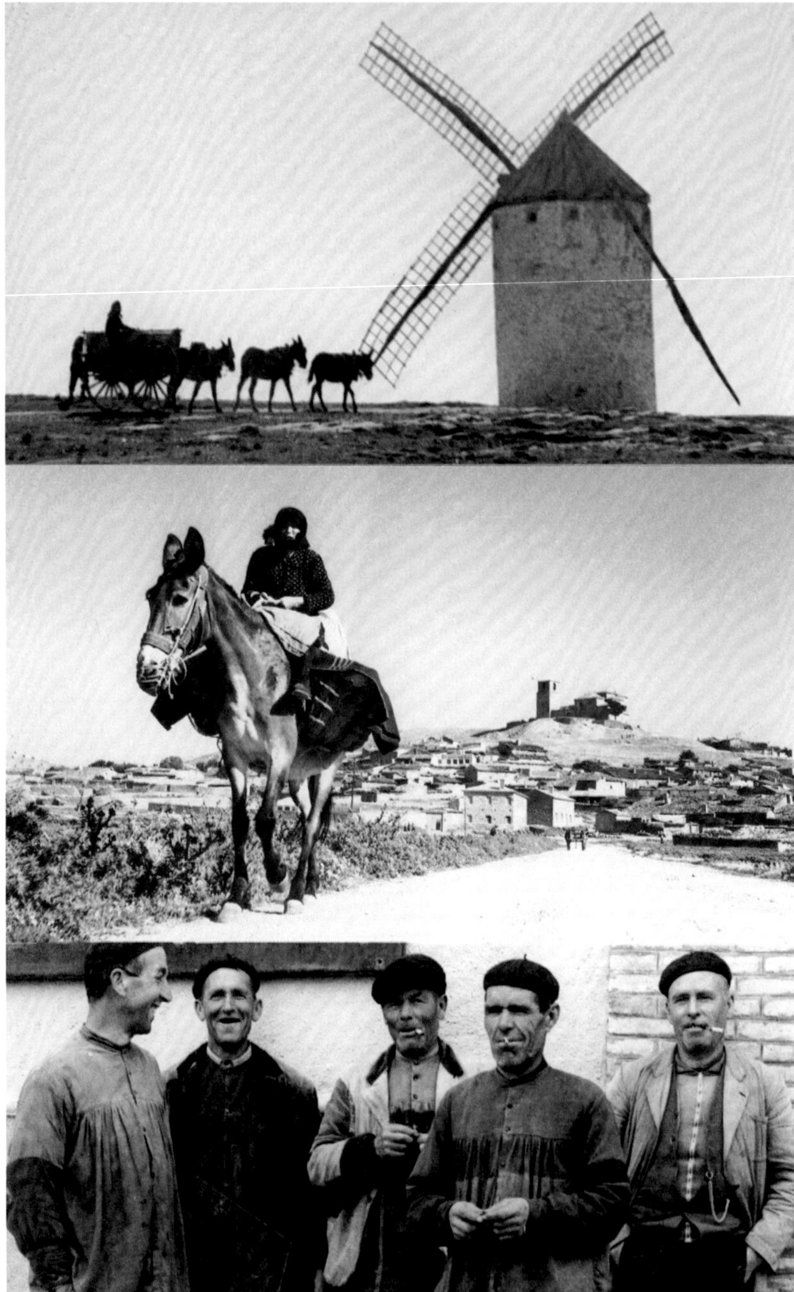

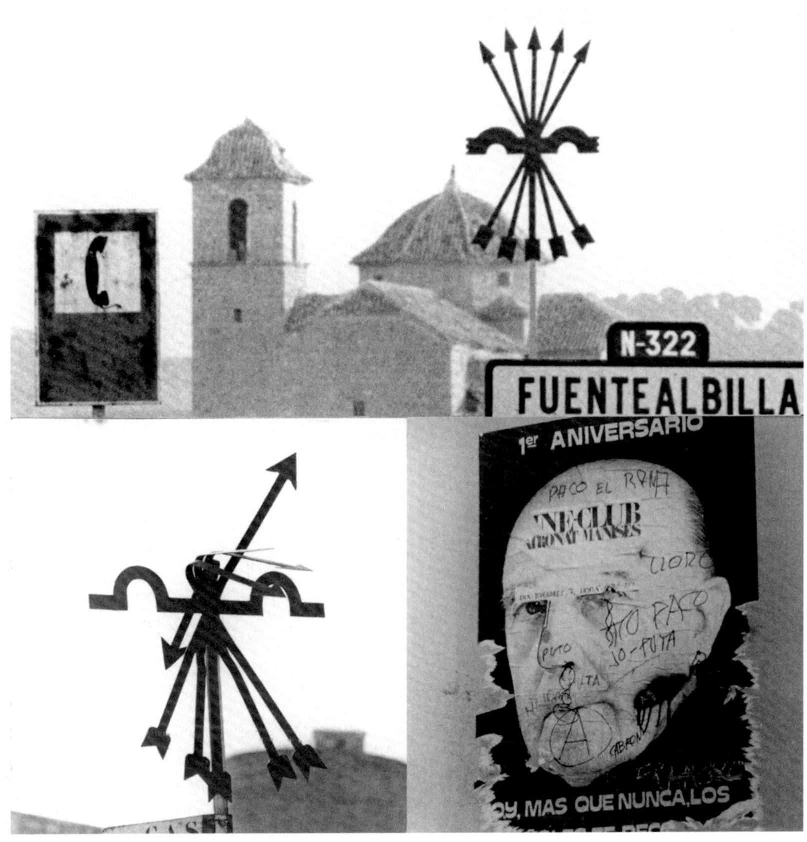

Peak and decline of the Francoist era.

On the previous page:
The Windmills of Campo de Criptana.
Moorish scene in Albadalejo del Cuende (Cuenca).
Characters from La Mancha.

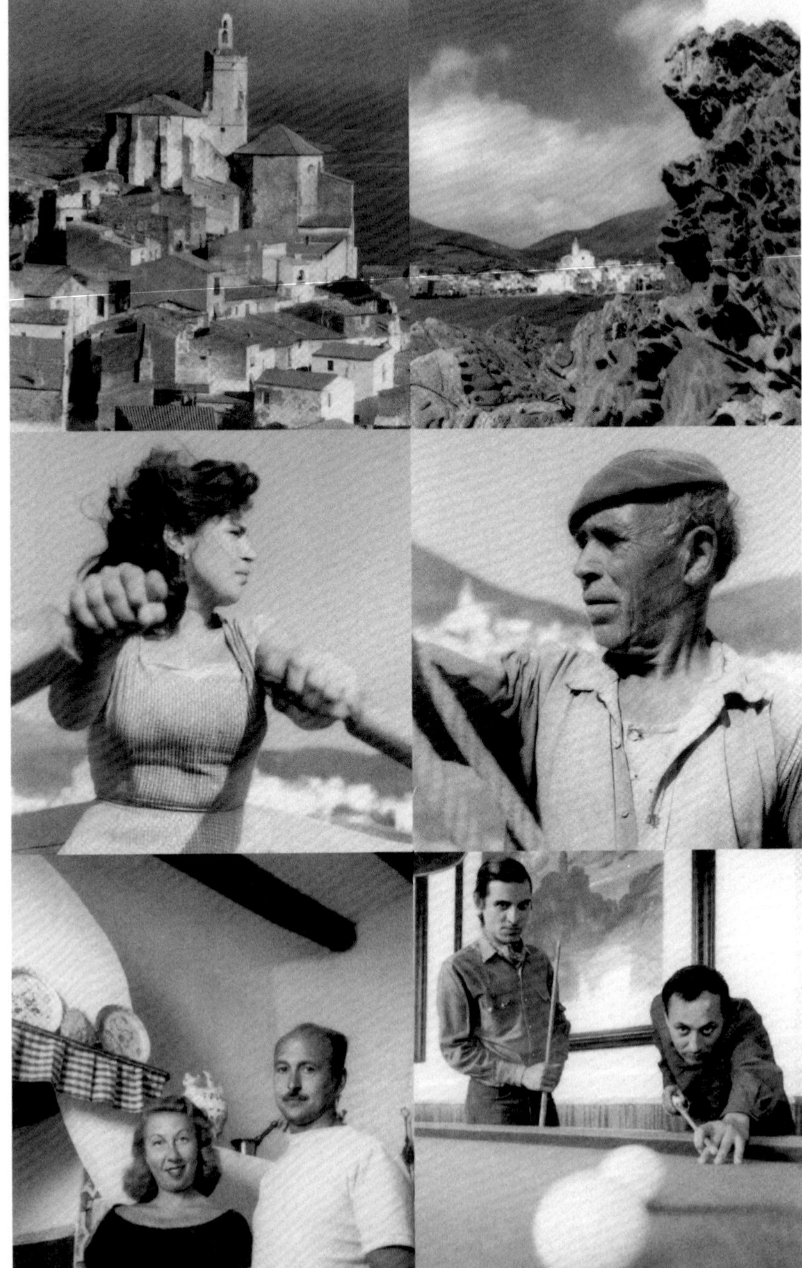

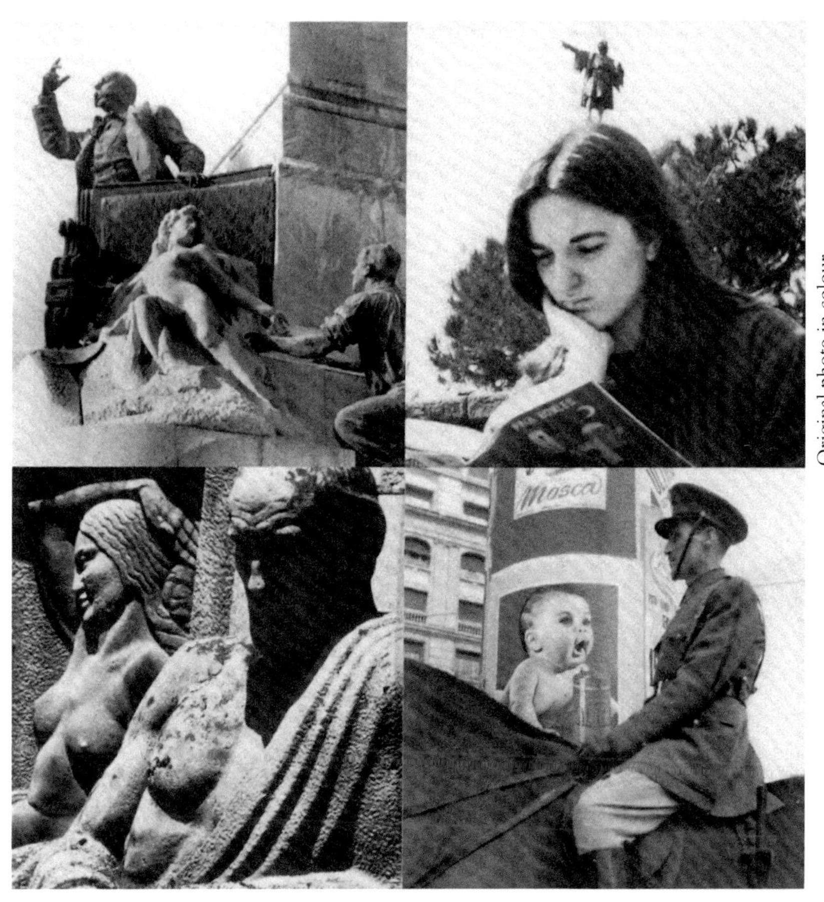

Monument to Castelar, on the Paseo de la Castellana in Madrid.
Monument to Columbus in Barcelona.
Monument to Ramón y Cajal in the Retiro Park in Madrid.
Advertising on the Gran Via in Barcelona.

On the previous page:
View of Cadaqués.
Two native characters.
Glòria and Lluís Romero, my family from Cadaqués.
Xavier Corberó and Joan Ponç at the Casino.

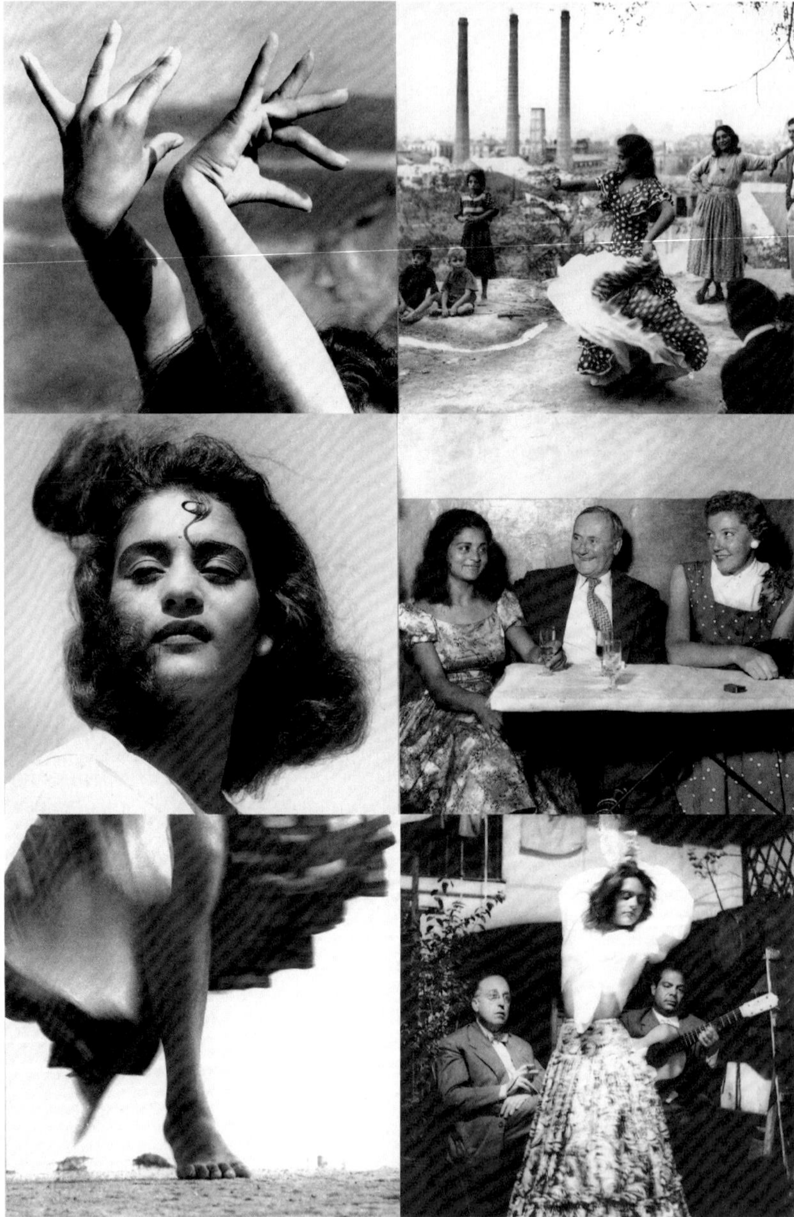

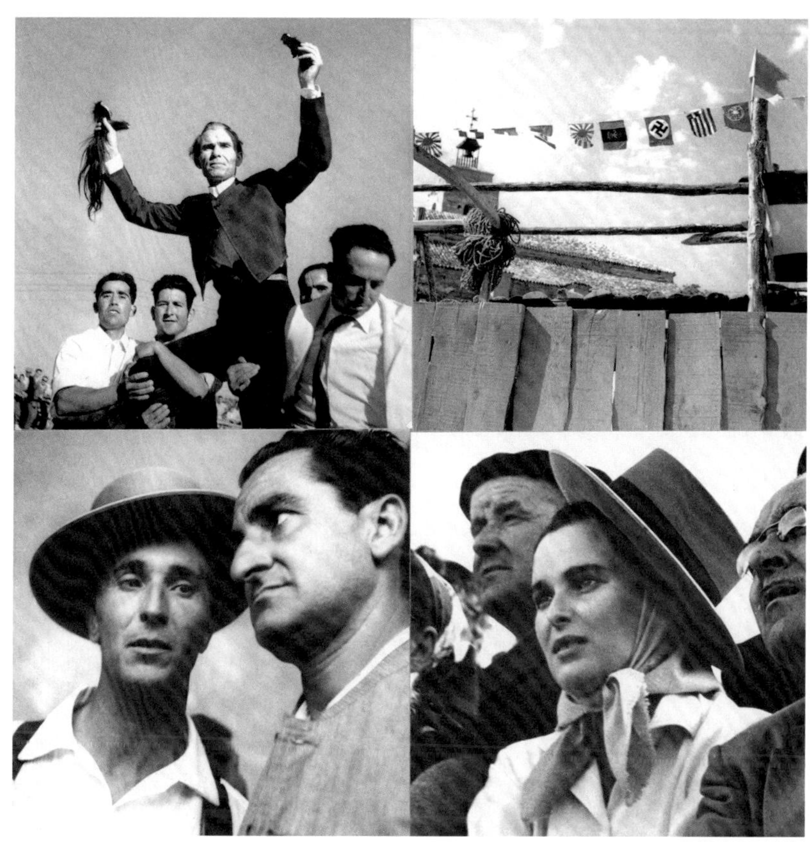

The festival in Carrascosa del Campo (Cuenca).
The triumph of Domingo Ortega.
The pennants of the Eix.
L. Miguel Dominguín and Bienvenida.
Lucía Bosé.

On the previous page:
La Chunga.
From Montjuïc.
Miró between La Chunga and Valerie, 'a brunette and a blonde.'
With Sebastià Gasch and Ramon, 'the fly man.

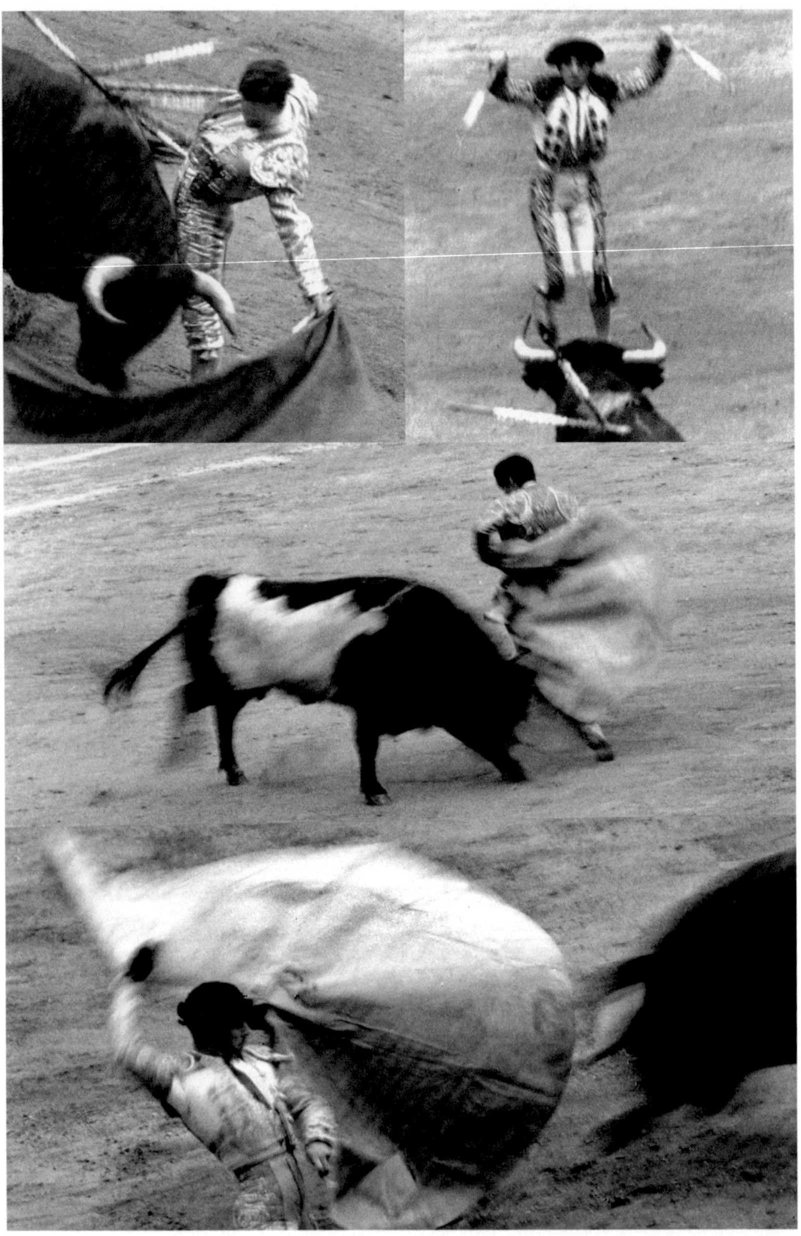

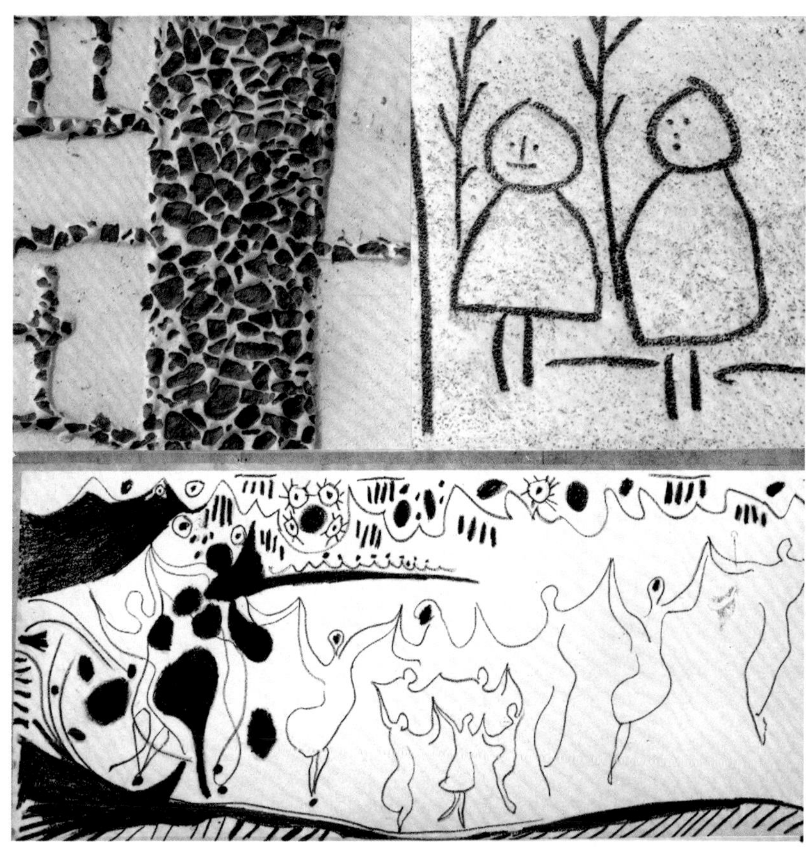

Picasso's works at the Architects' Association.
The Mironian sardana.

On the previous page:
Dynamic photos of bullfighting.
To give the sensation of movement in the image, some element must remain static.

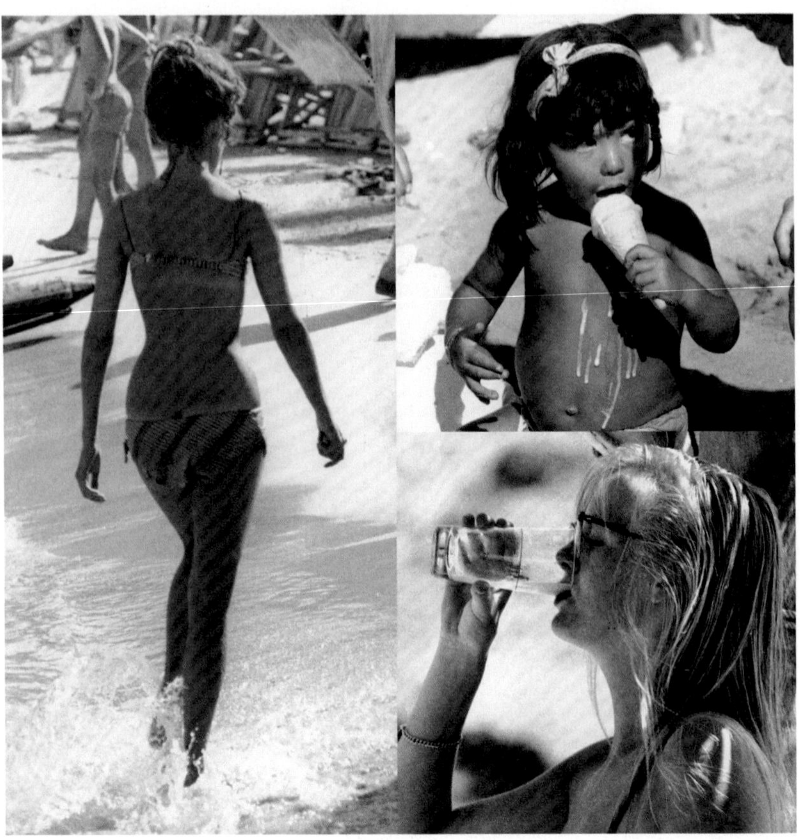

Promotional photos commissioned by the General Directorate of Tourism.

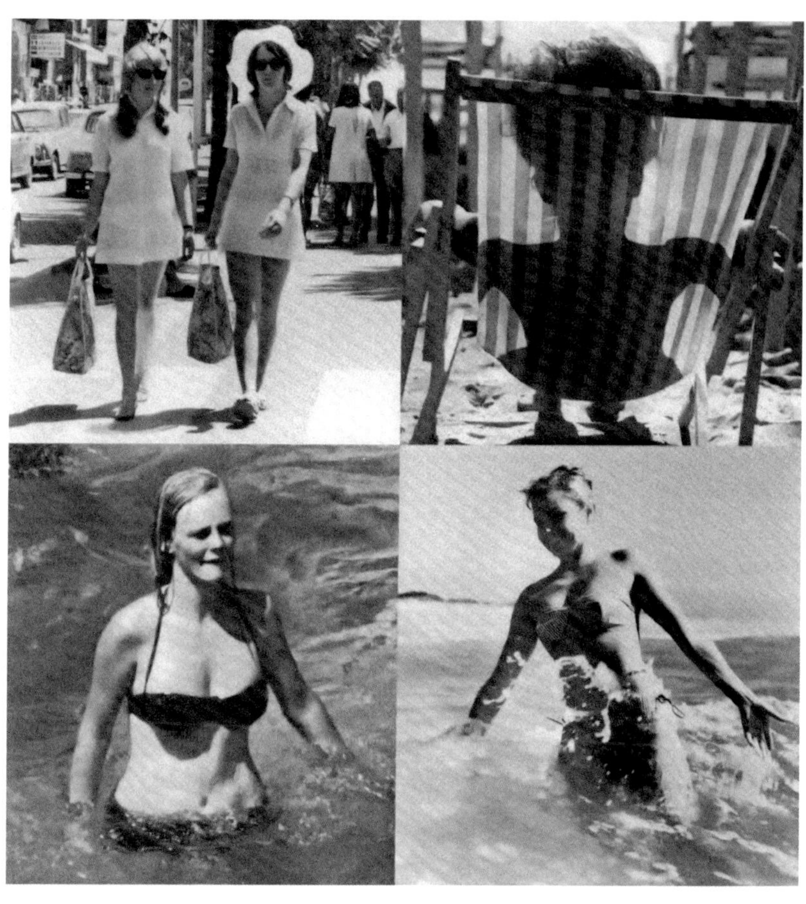

The arrival of Nordic tourists was shocking, and it made evident the backwardness we were experiencing here.

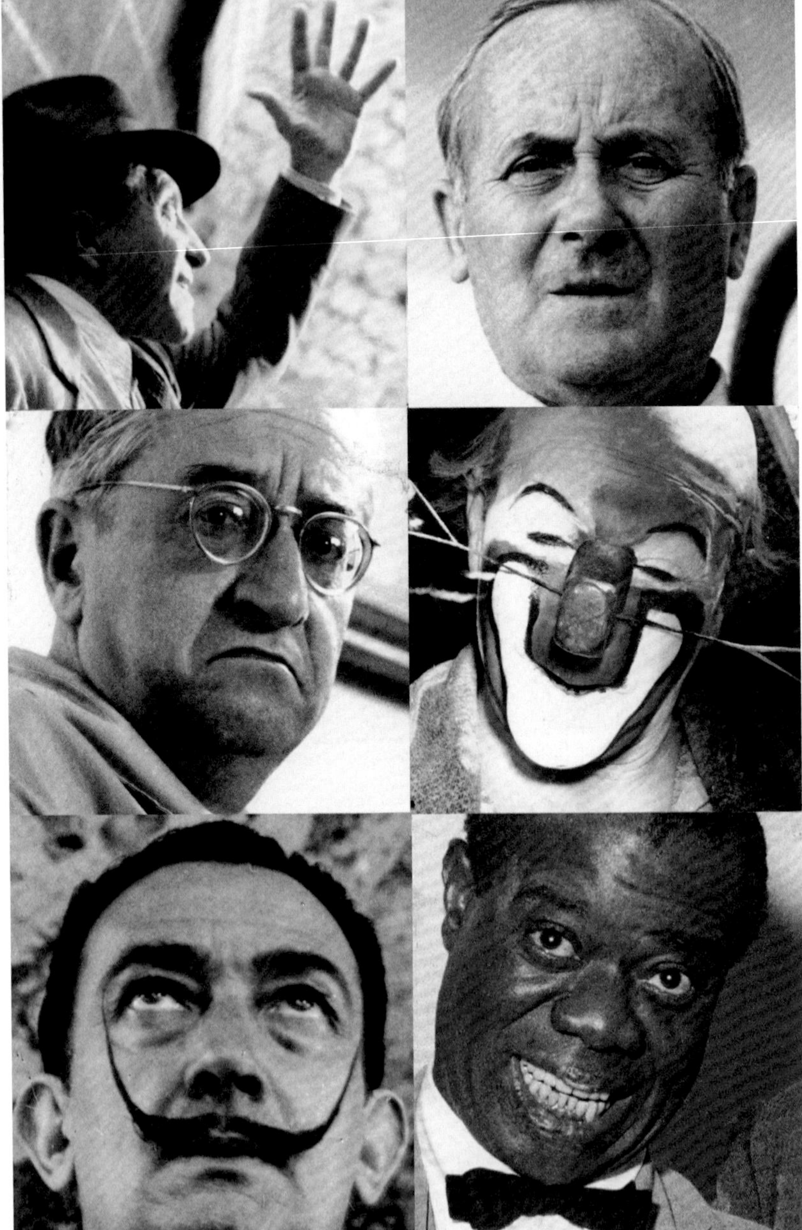

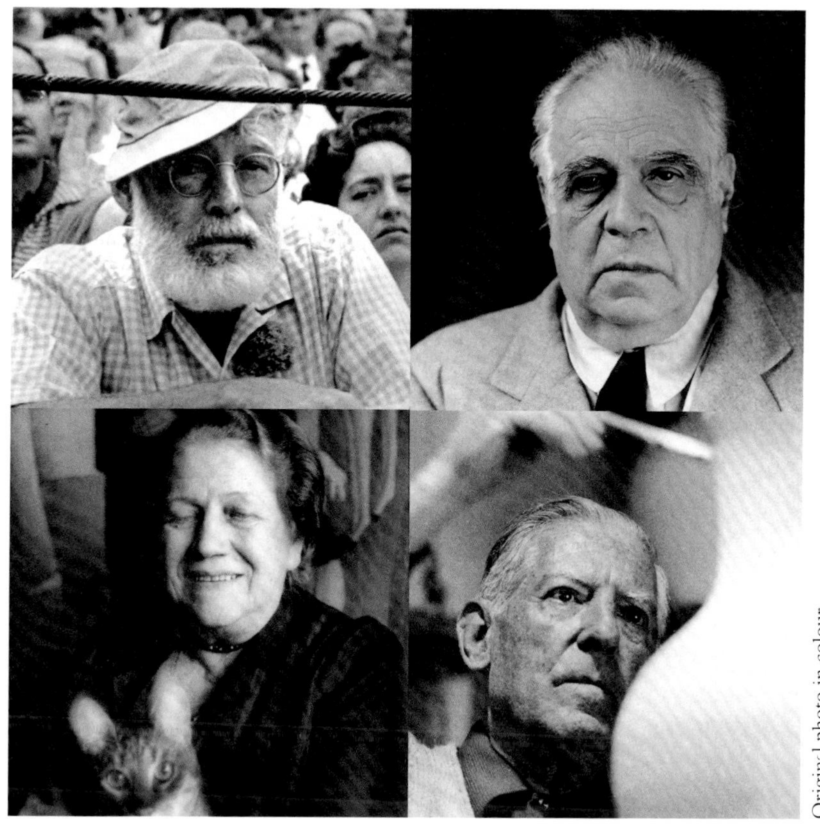

Original photo in colour

Ernest Hemingway, Eugeni d'Ors.
Olga Sacharoff. Josep Llorens Artigas.

On the previous page:
Joan Prats. Joan Miró.
Carles Riba. Charlie Rivel.
Salvador Dalí. Louis Armstrong.

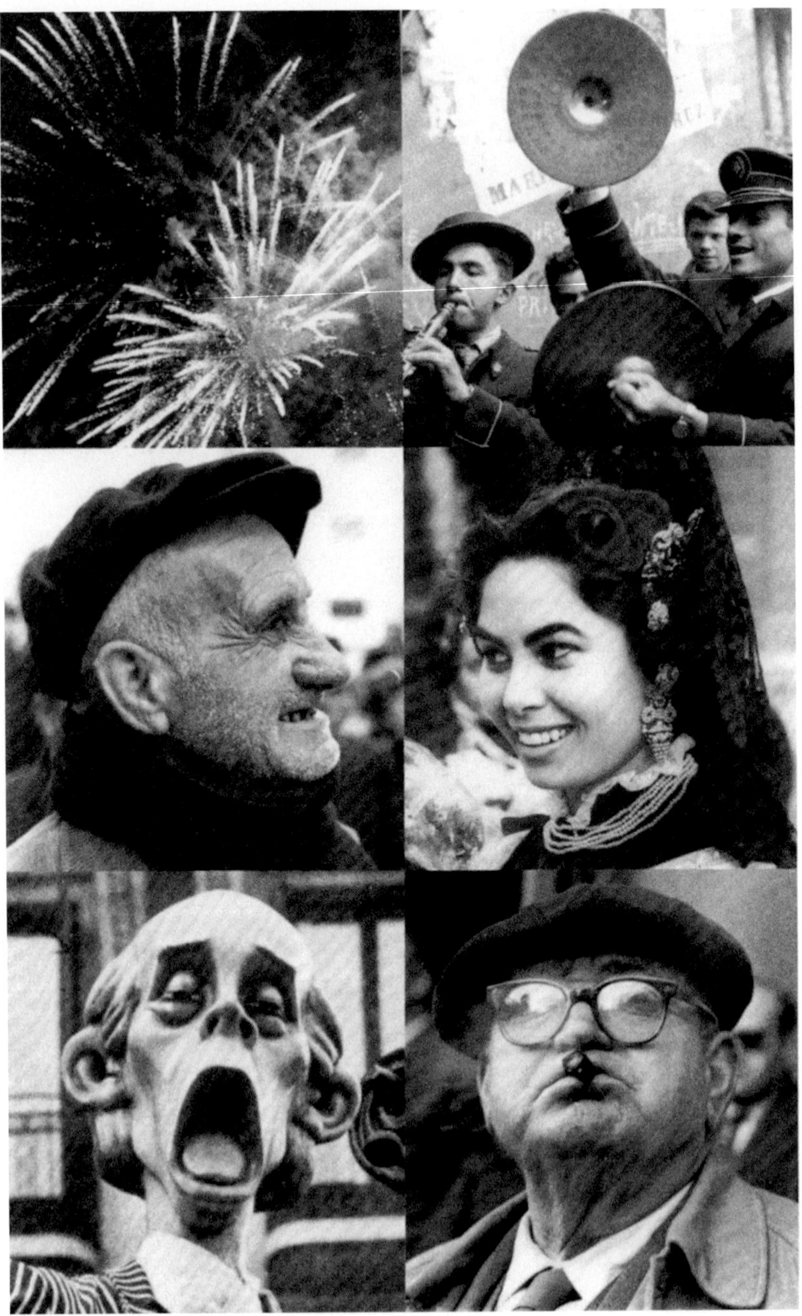

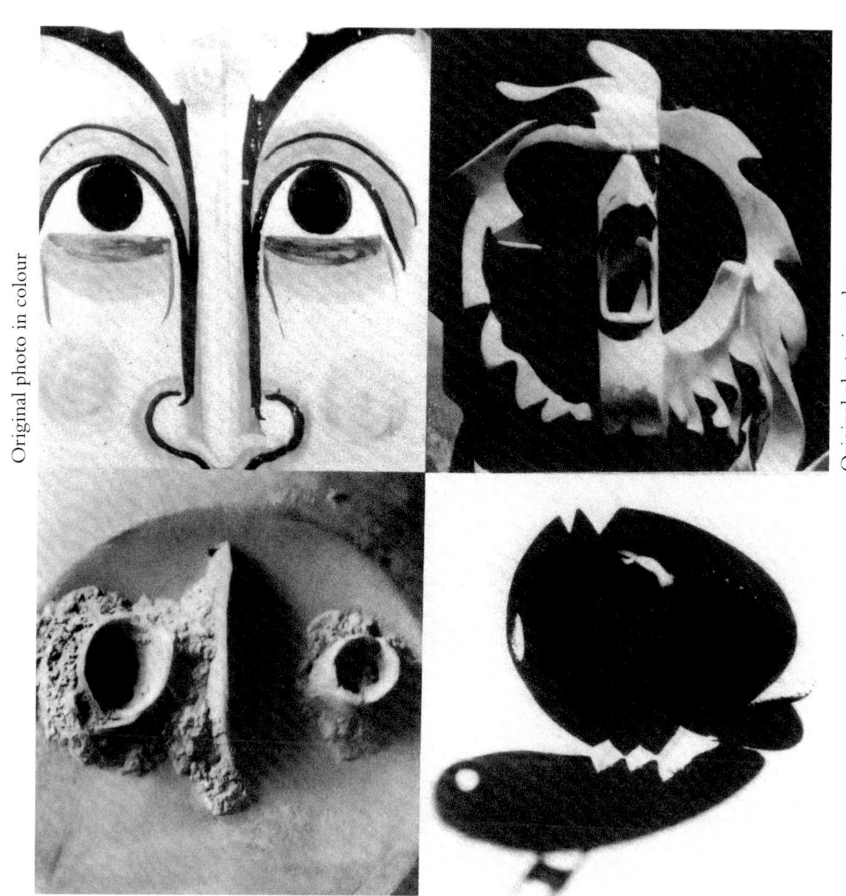

Pantocrator of Taüll.
Head of the Prophet by Pau Gargallo.
Bronze by Joan Miró.
Sculpture by Moisés Villèlia.

On the previous page:
Las Fallas of Valencia.
People who seem to have come out of the Fallas.

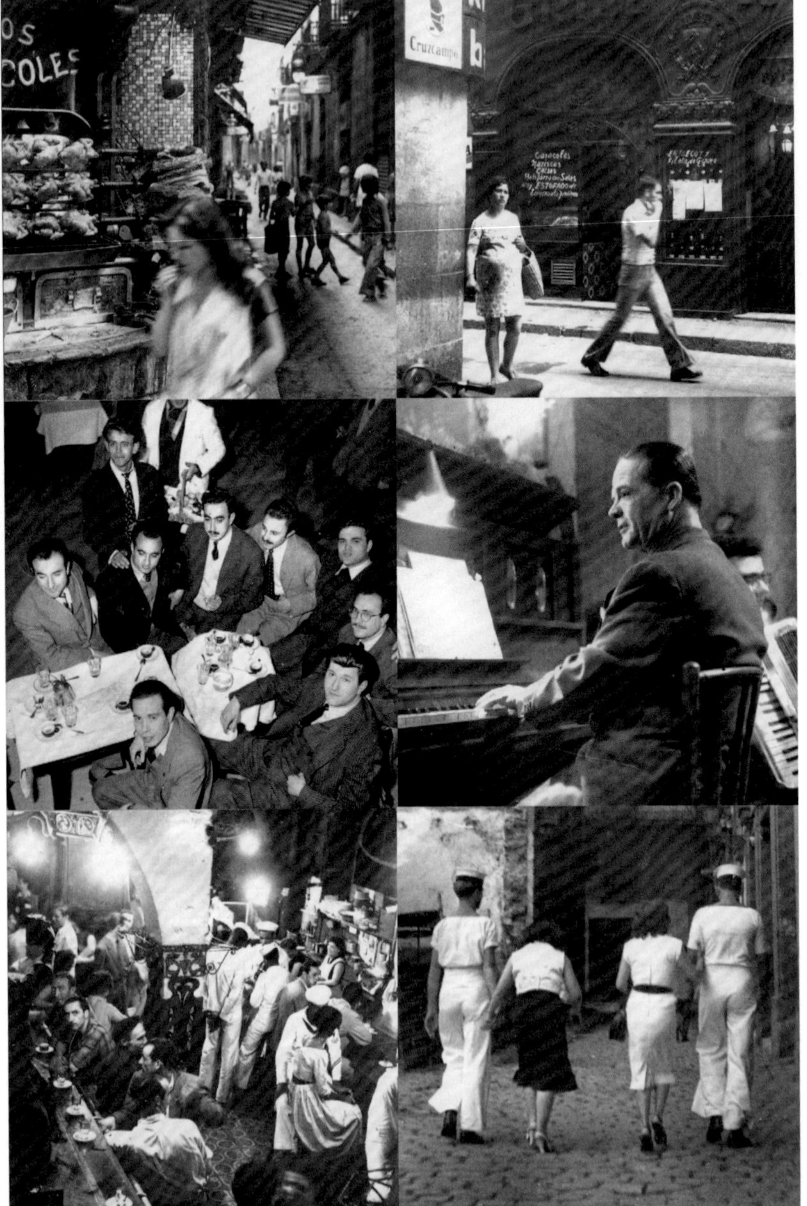

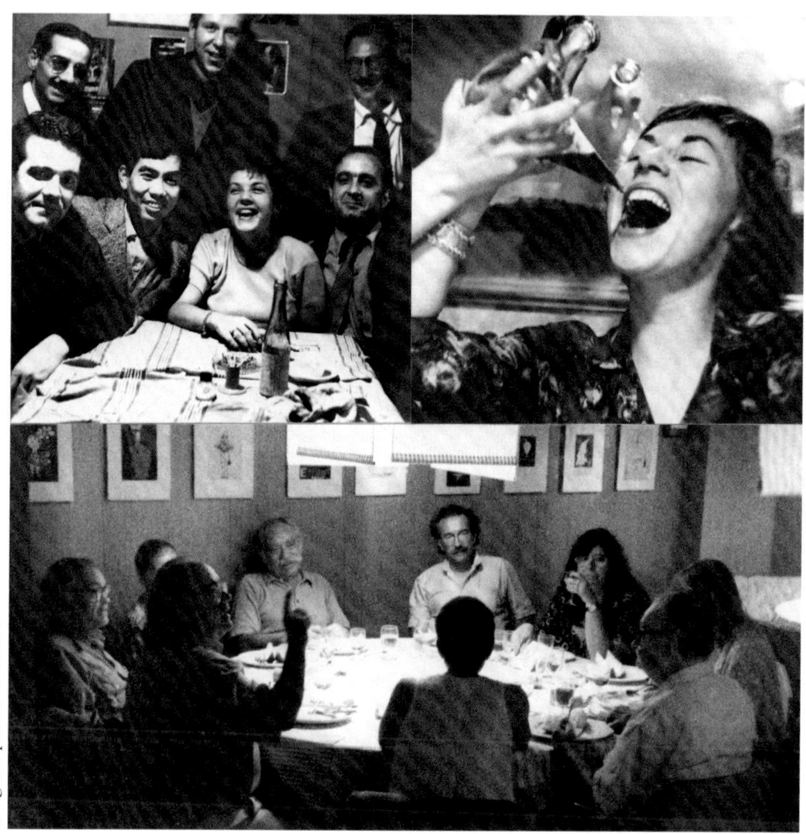

Photo at Casa Estevet (Ca la Mariona, for us).
Teaching a Swiss friend how to drink from a porró.
Tono Carrera took this photo of us at the Sí Senyor gathering.
Fausto, with his finger raised, is preparing a magic trick;
for now, he has already made Montserrat disappear.

On the previous page:
The neighborhood of Escudellers Street.
Modernist façade of the Grill Room.
The friends gathered: Cesáreo, Aleu, Poveda, J. Fornas, Guinovart, Balenyà,
Sobregrau and… standing, the pugilist, our admirer.
The pianist Miret.
Arrival of the Americans, one table for the sailors and the other for the locals.
'Friendship' has no borders.

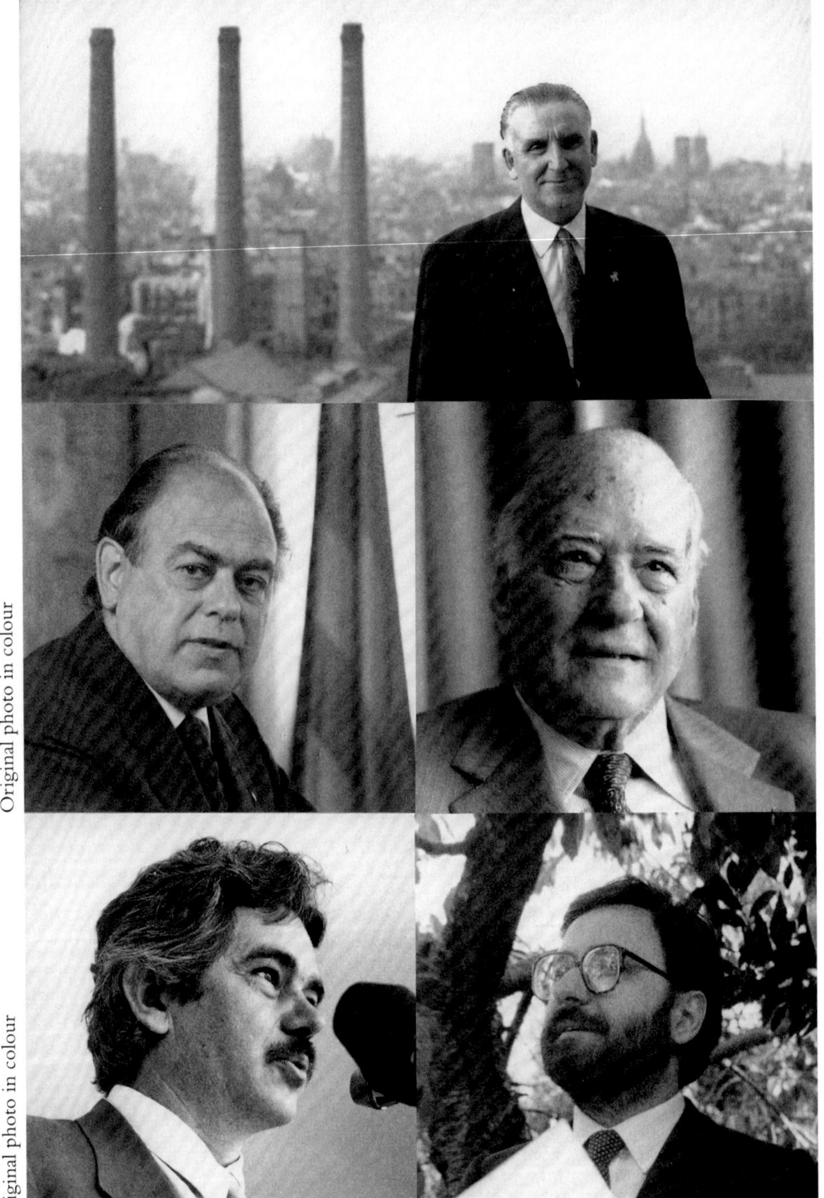

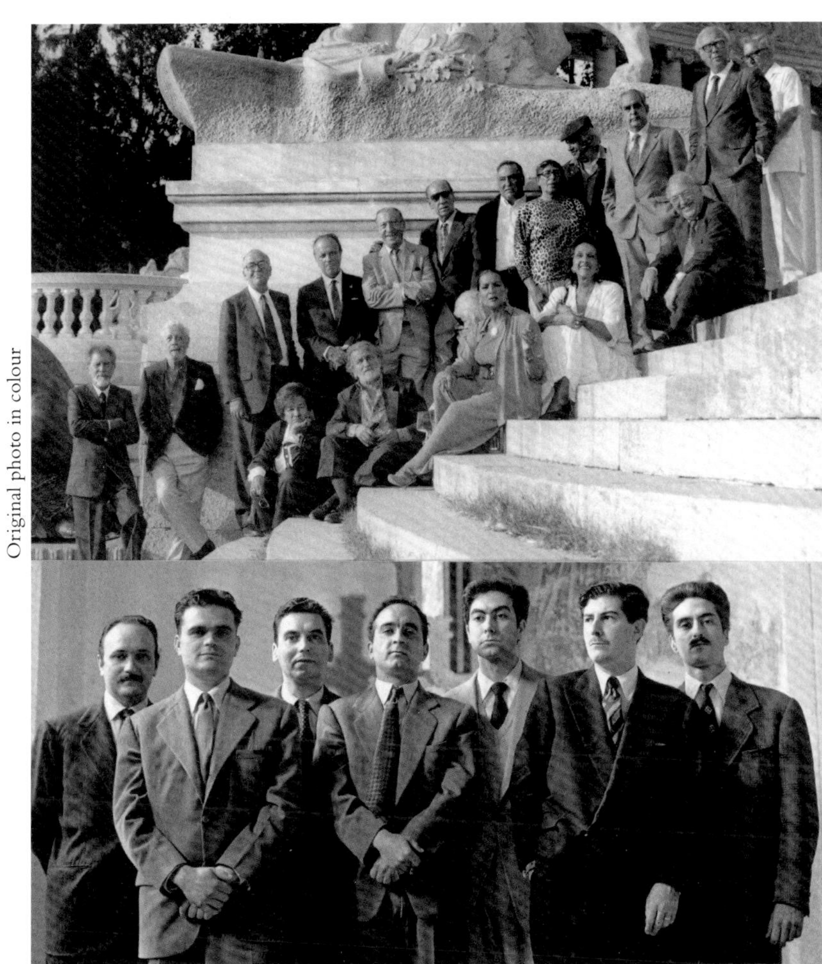

Group from the television program Los años vividos.
Group Taüll: Jaume Muxart, Josep Guinovart, Joan Josep Tharrats,
Marc Aleu, Antoni Tàpies, Modest Cuixart, and Jordi Mercadé.

On the previous page:
J.M. Porcioles.
Jordi Pujol. Josep Tarradellas.
Pasqual Maragall. Narcís Serra.

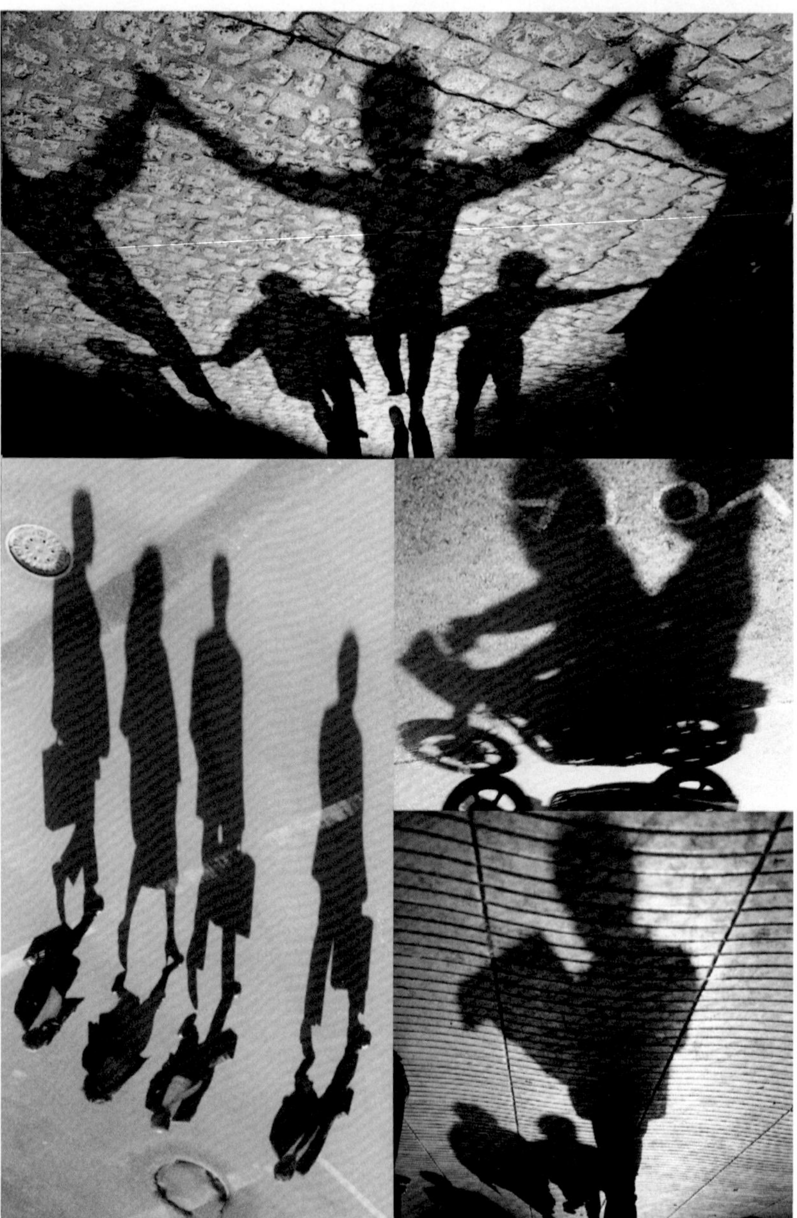

Original photos in colour

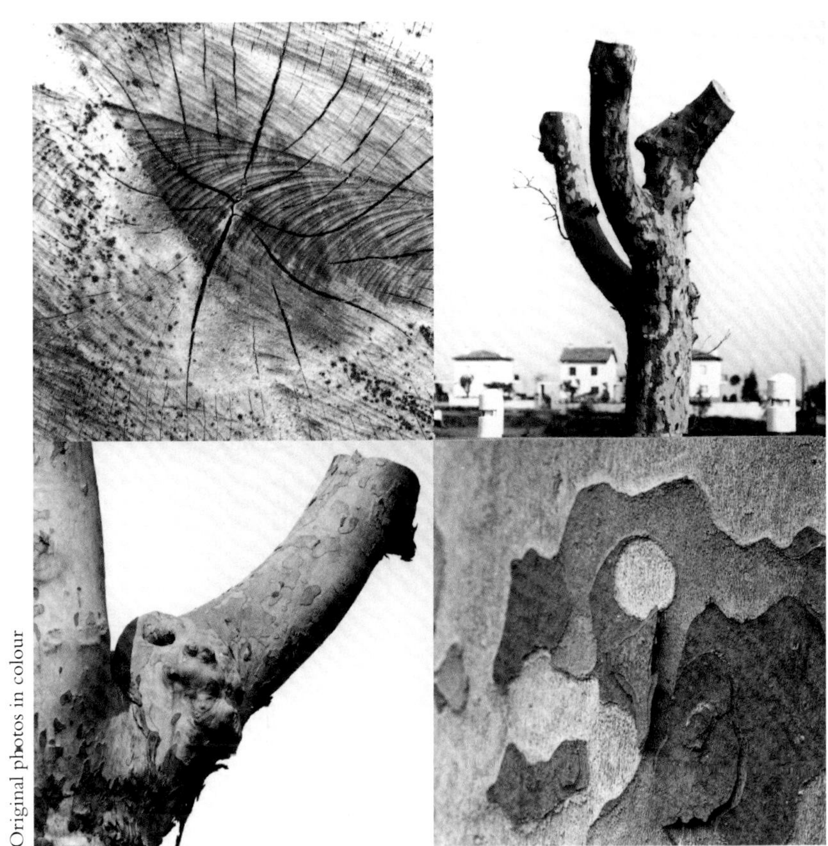

The pruning of the trees on the road from Sant Feliu de Codines, in Gallifa,
allowed me to publish a report in the newspaper La Vanguardia.

On the previous page:
The sun is a great photographer, creator of magnificent images.
Too bad it doesn't know how to fix them.

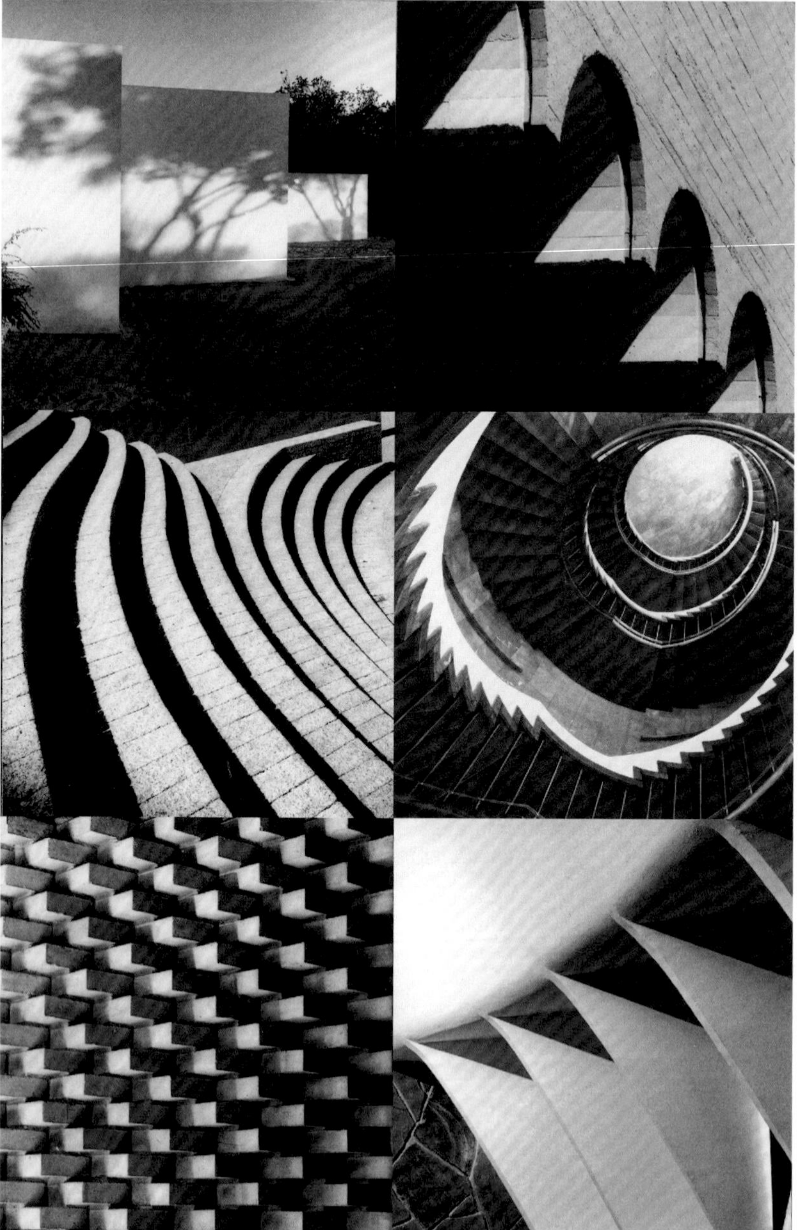

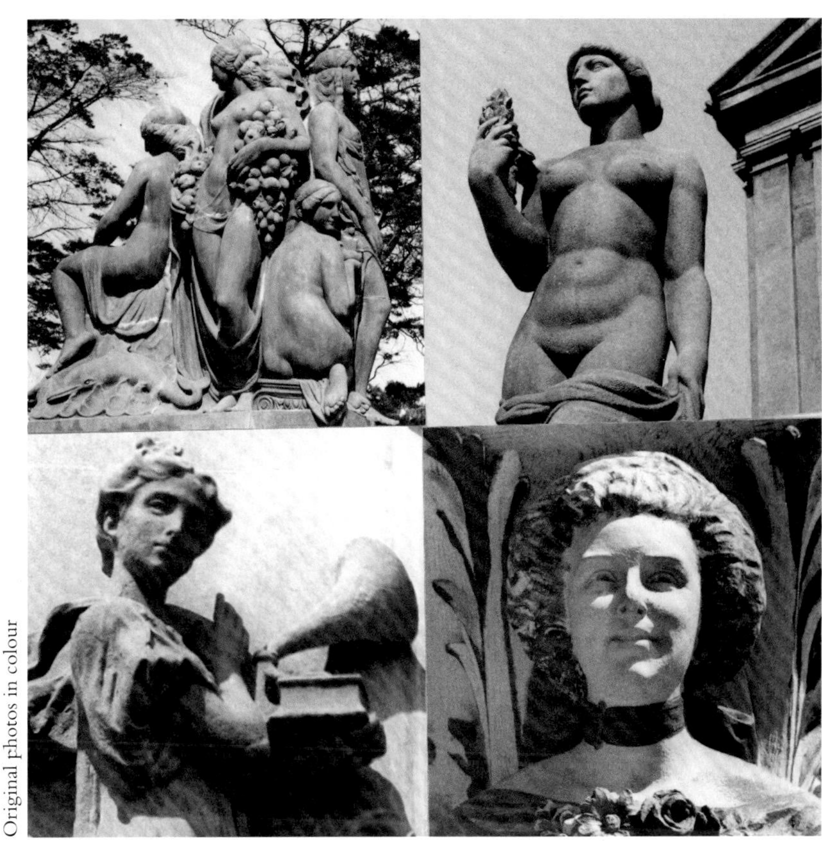

BARCELO-NINES.
Barcelona is full of sculptures depicting women.

On the previous page:
Architecture photos.
Coderch de Sentmenat. J. Ll. Sert.
Peña Ganchengui. Martorell-Bohigas.
Moragas Gallissà. Barba Corsini.

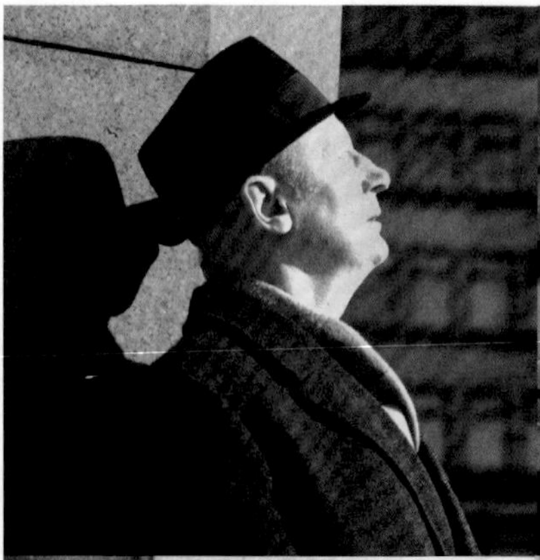

POHJOLA

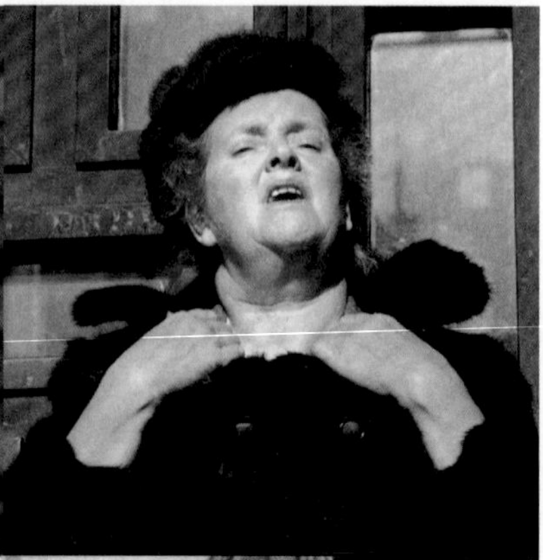

BUS STOP

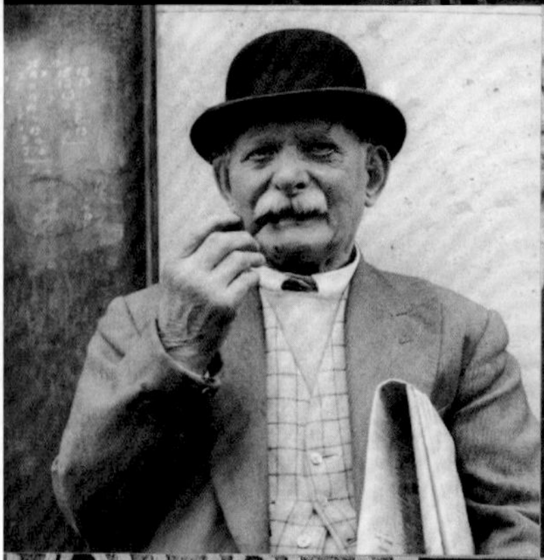

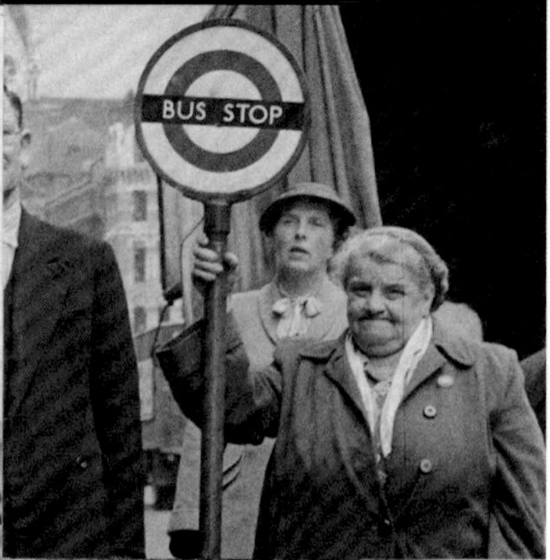

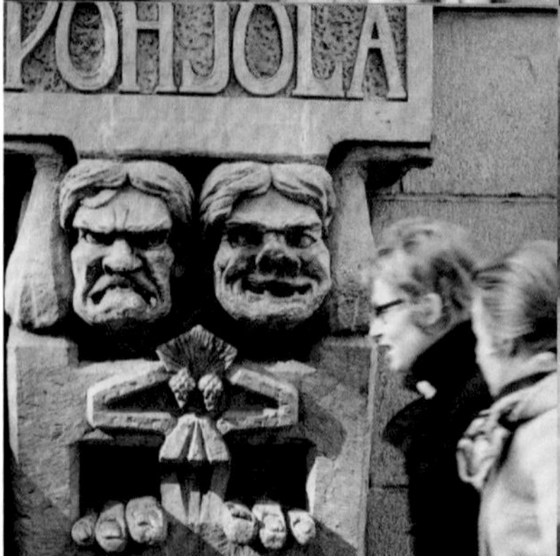

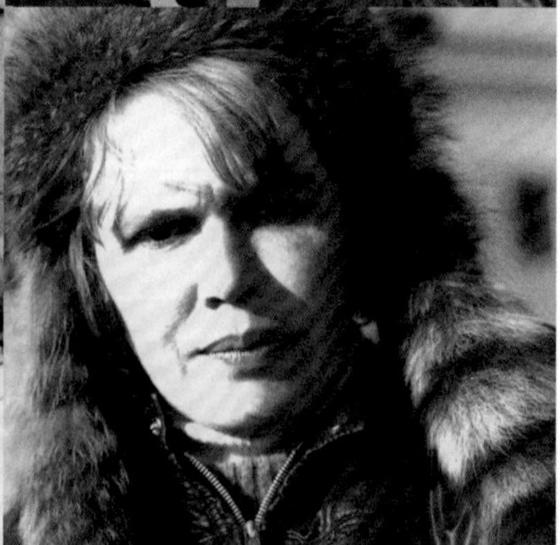

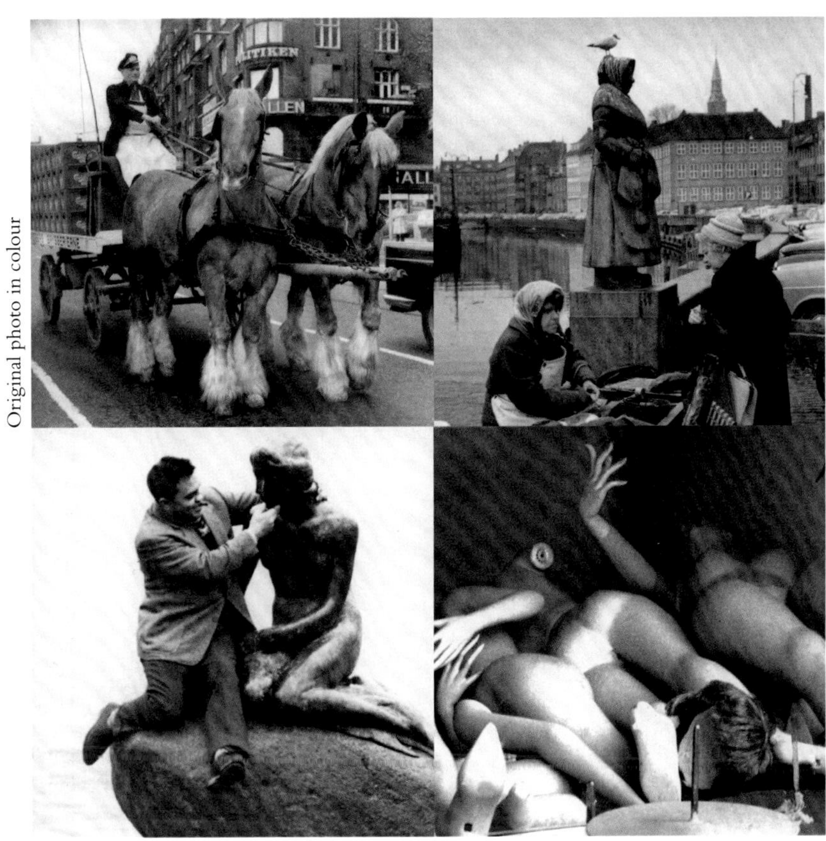

COPENHAGEN.
Beer delivery cart.
Fish market with its monument.
Me playing with the Little Mermaid.
Truck transporting mannequins that reminded me of the Nazi concentration camps.

On the previous page:
Traveling through Europe.
In Stockholm, characters thirsty for the sun.
In London, newspaper seller on Fleet Street, and a scene that reminded me
of Marilyn Monroe's movie Bus Stop.
In Helsinki, faces on the street, and a market seller.

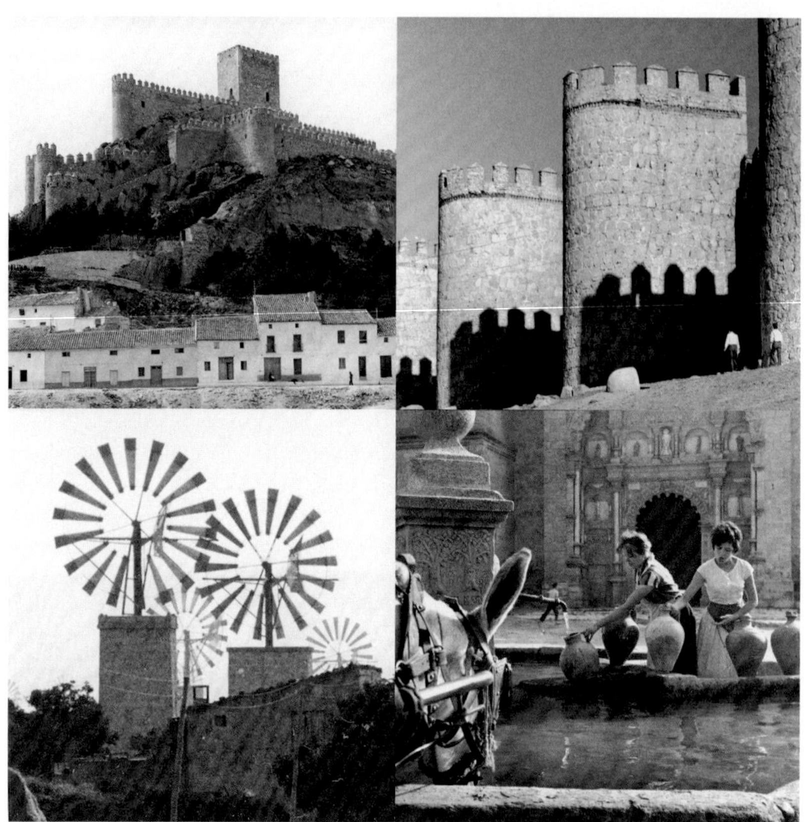

LANDSCAPES OF SPAIN.
Almansa Castle in Albacete.
Walls of Ávila.
Windmills of Mallorca.
Torrijos, province of Toledo.

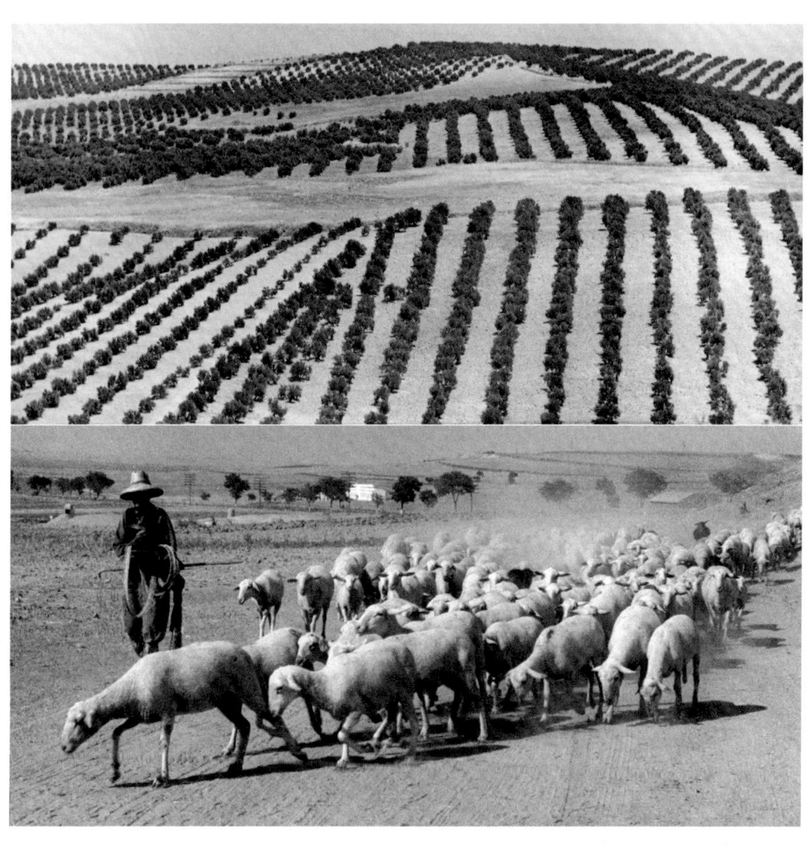

RURAL LANDSCAPES.
Olive trees in Jaén.
Livestock in Segovia.

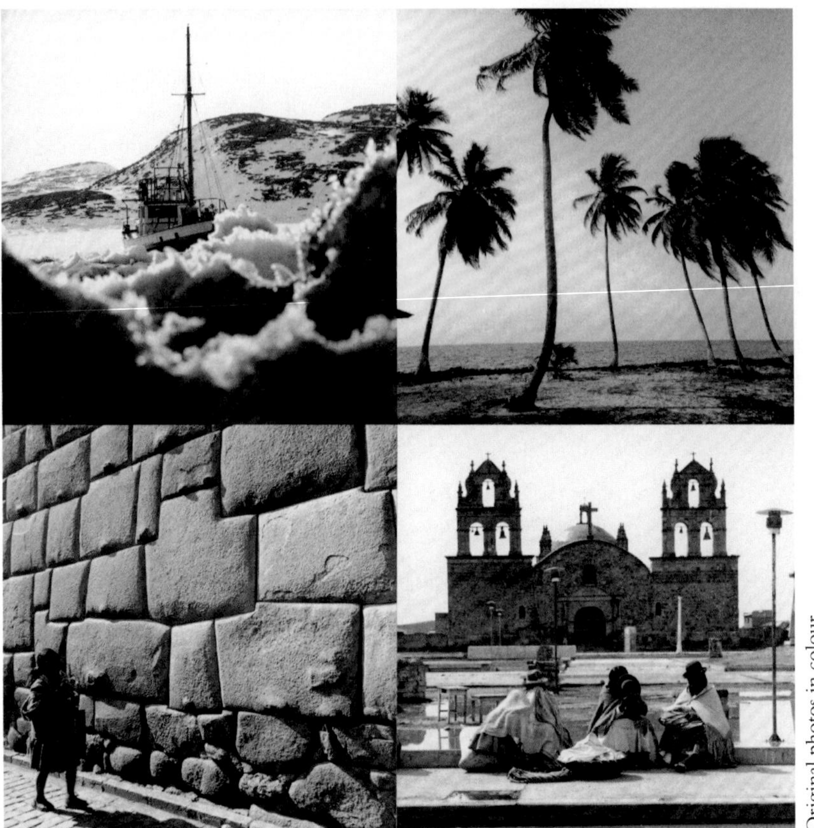

Original photos in colour

TRAVELING THROUGH AMERICA.
Panoramas of Alaska and the Caribbean.
Architecture of Cuzco (Peru) and the church of Laja (Bolivia).

On the next page:
Girl in a market in Mexico.
Inuit in Baffin Island (Canada).
Hat of great importance in Bolivia for the Spaniards.
With a load on the head, in Haiti.
Fur hat imitating the shape of the conquerors' helmets.
Mask for a festival in the Sierra de Nayarit (Mexico).

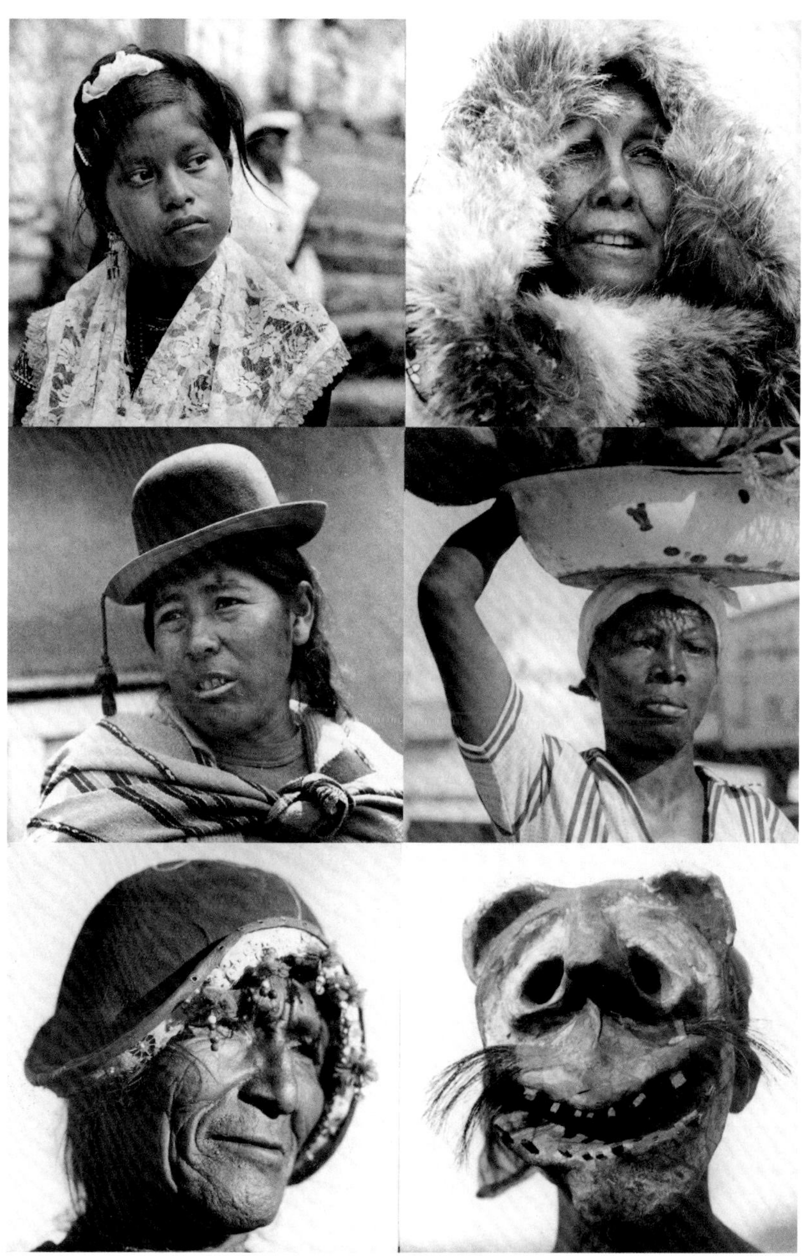

Original photos in colour

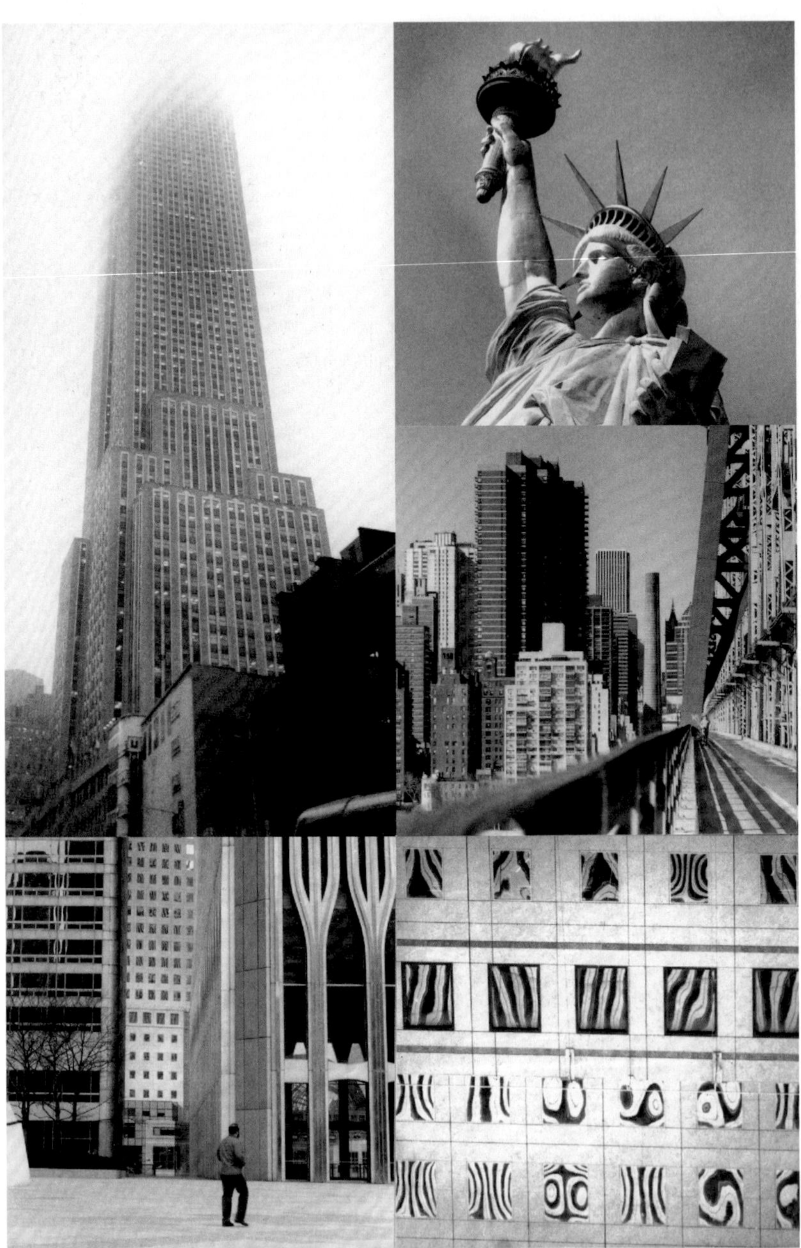

Original photos in colour

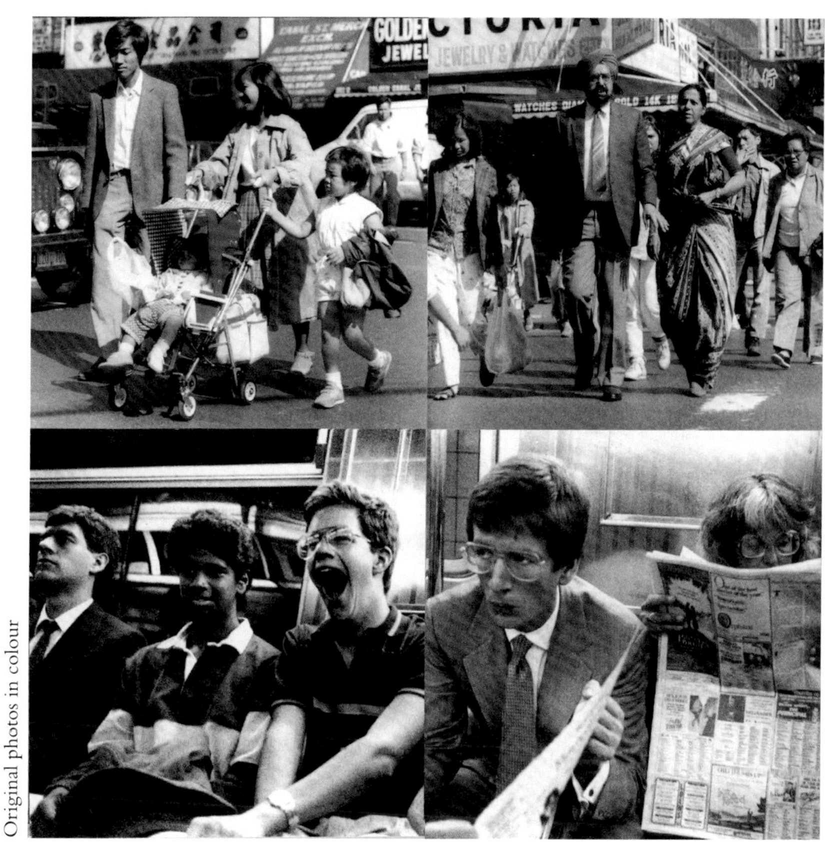

CITY PEOPLE.
Groups of Asians and Hindus.
Characters from the subway.

On the previous page:
MANHATTAN.
Photo explaining the reason for the word 'skyscraper.'
Symbol of New York.
Enlargement of the Windows where the Trade Towers are reflected.

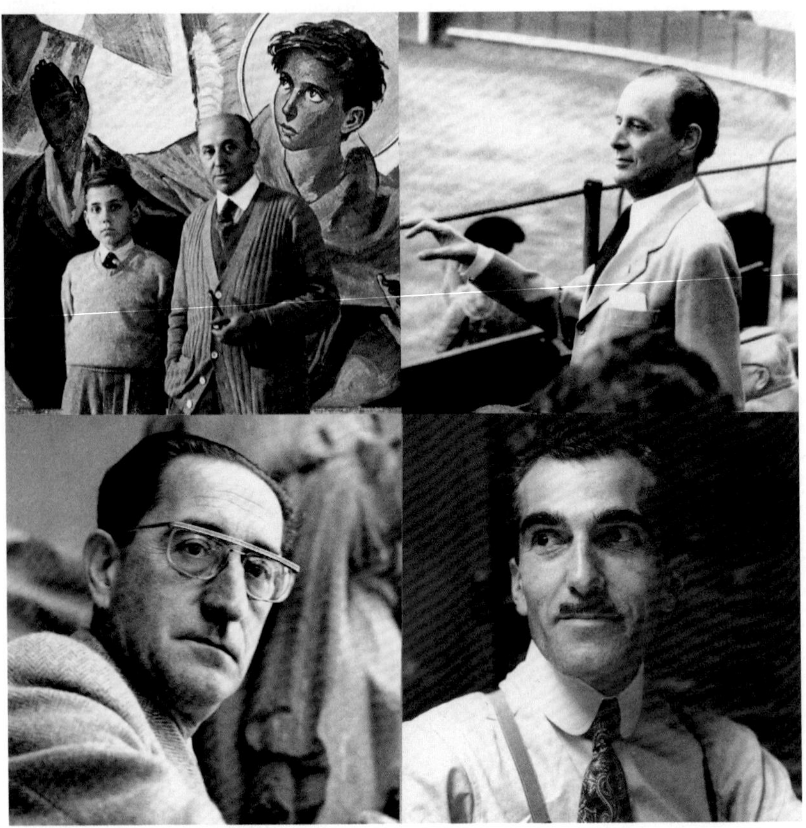

The painter Josep Obiols with his son Raimon, who served as his model.
Albert Puig Palau, founder of Revista *and a great fan of bullfighting.*
From the Destino publishing house, Joan Teixidor created many illustrated books with photographs.
Ricard Giralt-Miracle, Master of graphic design and creator of Filograf.

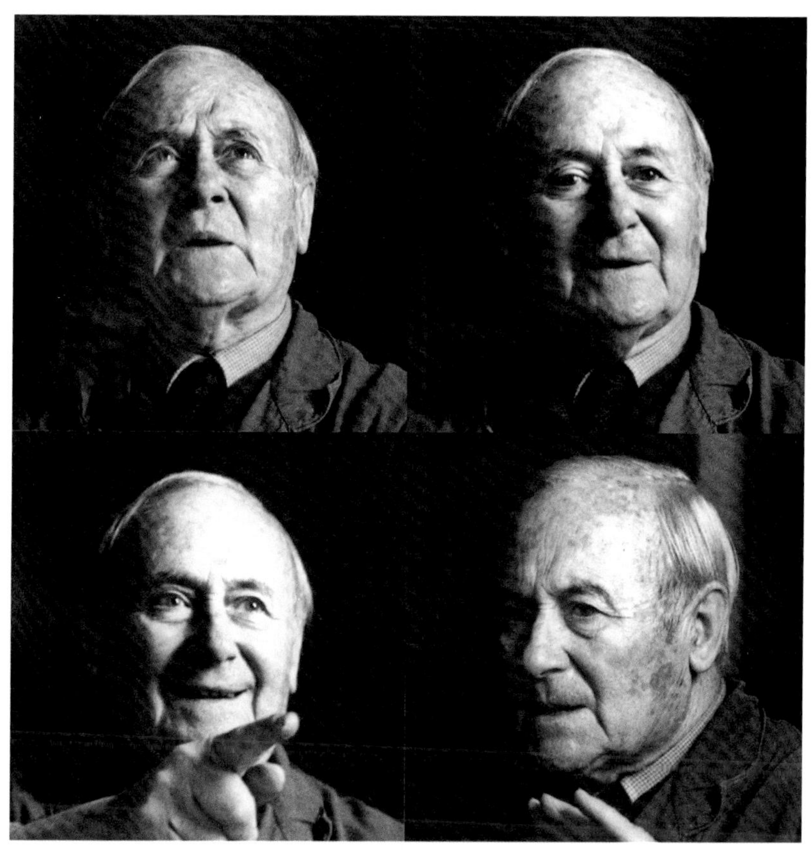

The persistence of images in memory creates animation.
That's why, if you spend a moment looking at these portraits, you'll get
the feeling that Miró is moving.

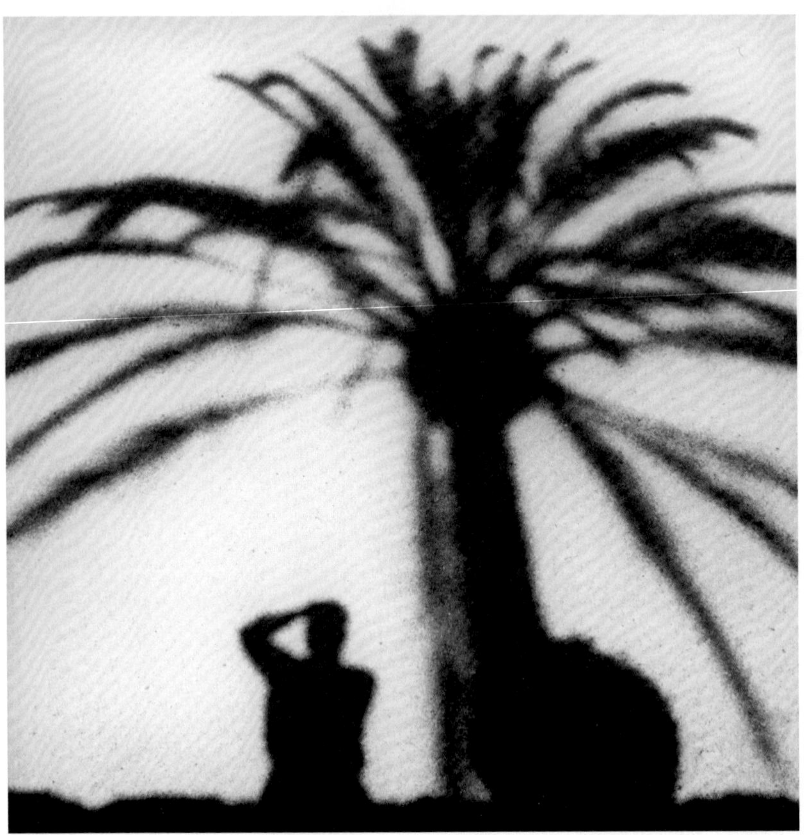

As a creator of images, the sun remains the great master.
From a simple palm tree in the Park Güell, it is capable of creating this beautiful
graphic design, which the photographer only needs to capture.

he still had the presence of mind to say they would talk about it
after lunch because it was time to eat, but of course, Artigas knew
perfectly well that the painting had just been sold. With the passing
of the years, in his old age Artigas started to lose his memory. His
two children, Joanet and especially Mariette, took very good care
of him. It was Joanet who carried on the collaboration with Miró
after his father's death, and together they set up what is now the
Llorens Artigas Foundation, which for anyone who cares about art
amply justifies a trip to Gallifa.

What can I say about Japan? I went there, of course, to take
photographs of a commission that Miró and Artigas were working
on in the city of Osaka —a large ceramic mural, the components of
which they had made in Gallifa. I went there with Joanet Artigas
and they pretended that I was Japanese, albeit a mute, mentally
challenged Japanese, because I couldn't communicate with anyone.
On that occasion we were there because an access ramp to the
mural had to be painted —a ramp that Miró destroyed when the
exhibition closed, and so my photographs are the only surviving
evidence of it. Later, when the official inauguration of Miró's work
was to take place, I went to Osaka again. On this visit they gave me
an interpreter who spoke very good Spanish and was passionate
about flamenco and bullfighting, on account of which I called him
Paco de Osaka. He was the first to tell me about the guitarist Paco
de Lucía, and one night he invited me to a *tablao* (the Japanese
pronounced it 'taburao') where I met the dancer Sara Lezama.
On the day of the opening, I was particularly struck by the way
the people lined up to see the pavilions, and especially the Gas
Pavilion, in which there was the large mural by Miró and Artigas.
The Japanese have always loved Miró's art, and although they had
to queue for hours to see the mural there was no fuss: they simply
squatted down with their arms around their knees and waited!
I was greatly impressed by the Japanese when I saw how they
lived and worked. Always in small spaces, but very well organised
and very practical, always sitting on the floor and with extremely

precise rules of conduct and protocol, in marked contrast to our Western ways of seeing and doing things.

Carles Riba

During my time at *Revista* I was sent to do a photographic report on the poet Carles Riba and his wife Clementina Arderiu, also a poet, who were being given a house by Cadaqués Town Council. This event brought together a considerable number of figures from the Catalan literary scene –Sagarra, Soler Vicens, Tomàs Garcés, Rosa Leveroni, Granyer, Dr Trueta and a long list of others– around the two poets. One of the photos I took was of the mirror in the bar in which the official ceremony took place, which reflected many of the faces of the throng. A little later I took more shots, of Riba and Arderiu entering their new home in Cadaqués with the keys in their hands, and then even more photos of the couple sitting at the dining table, as if they had been ensconced there for a while… Finally, I took one of Carles Riba alone, with a book. I must say that I have a very good memory of this photo-essay, which was published in *Revista*, because it is one of those occasions when a good part of the Catalan intelligentsia could be seen together.

Some time after that I had an exhibition at Sala Caralt (this would have been in the early fifties), and I wanted to include a whole section of portraits, seven in particular, one of which was a photograph of Carles Riba. This section was so successful that everyone wanted me to make a portrait of them, but of course I told them that I never did portraits as such; that those were not real portraits, because I had done them without the individuals portrayed having asked me to. I have never liked to do portraits or personalised photographs to commission, as I have always been more interested in portraying people in the place and time of my choosing. In the same exhibition there was also a photograph of the clown Charlie Rivel, and quite apart from the fact that Carles and Charlie are the same name I consider the two photos to have much in common, in that one was the personification of the drama and the other the personification of the comic.

Thomas Bouchard

He was, without a doubt, one of the greatest influences on my
professional career and at the same time one of those who have
had the greatest influence on both the world of photography and
the world of cinema. In the fifties, the famous journalist Manolo
del Arco's interviews of interesting personalities were a regular
feature in the daily paper *La Vanguardia*. In order to find out if a
figure of some importance had arrived in Barcelona, he cultivated
contacts in the city's hotels, who would let him know if they had
any important guests. One day he recieved a call from the Hotel
Colón to inform him that they had an American staying there
(who seems to have been the first such guest they ever had). Del
Arco got in touch with the man, and asked what had brought him
to Barcelona. And Bouchard told him that he had come to make
a film about Miró. I read the interview and was very interested,
of course, as he was in the world of cinema and documentaries, I
resolved to meet him. In the newspaper interview Bouchard had
mentioned Joan Prats, and as Prats was a friend of my father, I
immediately went to see him and asked him to put me in touch
with the American. However, Prats had no interest in my request
and did nothing at all to help me. At that time, I had already
made my first film, about the Sagrada Família, which I entered
to the Ciutat de Barcelona awards (and won). I used to go buy
photographic and cinematographic materials at a shop on Carrer
de Sant Pau —Alexandre— and one day they suggested that I put
on a screening of my film in the same shop. And so we did, after it
closed for the day. After watching the film with a group of friends
and acquaintances, the owner of the shop, Daniel Aixela, told me
that a man who had come in to buy some materials and had heard
about the screening had asked to stay to see it, and now wanted
to meet me. That person was none other than Thomas Bouchard,
whom I was delighted to meet, and who warmly congratulated
me on my documentary. He told me about the Miró film he was
preparing to shoot and asked if I was interested in acting as his
assistant. My goodness! What a stroke of luck! I accepted at once,

of course. The very next day we met at his hotel to make the first work plans. I set aside the job I had been working at on to dedicate myself exclusively to this collaboration with Bouchard, thanks to which I got to know Miró and Pepito Artigas. Through Bouchard I also met Sert, whom we went to see in Palma, as at that time he was finishing the studio he was building for Miró. One afternoon we went for a walk and found ourselves at the cathedral. It was a quiet afternoon and when we went inside there seemed to be no one there but the two of us. Just then, someone began to play the organ. Bouchard, who was a great music lover, recognised the music, which was by Béla Bartók. It was quite inconceivable, at that time, to hear Bartók's music being played in Spain, and all the more so on the organ of Palma's impressive cathedral. I went to look for the organist, but was unable to find my way. Suddenly the music stopped and a few moments a priest appeared, who turned out to be the organist. I introduced him to Bouchard and they became great friends; while we were in Palma we met several times for dinner and he introduced us to his friends and fellow musicians.

During Bouchard's stay in Barcelona, I would go to seek him out at a bar next to the Hotel Colón. This bar reached almost down to the street, and one day when we were there he said to me: 'Now you will see a carriage with a prince pass by; he will blow his horn and all the princesses will come to bring him gifts.' Not long after he said this, the big rubbish truck arrived. The bin collector was a well-built young fellow wearing a sash and a cap, as was still customary at that time. He blew his trumpet and the maids from all the houses came out to bring him the rubbish. Bouchard saw the scene in his own way, with the eyes of his imagination.

The film about Miró was made entirely by Bouchard and me; once the filming was completed, he went to the United States to edit it, and returned to present and premiere it here. We did this at the Windsor cinema and then screened it in various places around the country (the Miró Foundation has a copy of the film). How things have changed in this regard. When Bouchard and I made that documentary, it was just the two of us working on it;

now, to make a documentary, even just for television, you need a whole team of people —and sometimes it shows in the results! They may not make any mistakes, but neither are they brilliant either, and the result is invariably mediocre.

Salvador Dalí

I mentioned Dalí's presence and involvement in the launch and the editing of *Revista*, a circumstance which was possible because Puig Palau was also a good friend of his. I had to make a reproduction of the masthead that Dalí drew, and that was what enabled me to get to know him and in due course to become his friend. He was a personage who liked above all to be talked about… even if they spoke well of him, as he used to say. During some of his stays in Cadaqués, at Portlligat, I went up there to take photographs of him. One of the shots I am most pleased and satisfied with is of Dalí with the *Corpus Hypercubus*. And I must honestly say that when I used to go there to photograph him, he tended not to act the divine Dalí, but behaved in a completely natural way. And what is more, he used to give me photographic advice. Let us not forget that Dali is the author of two of the very few theoretical texts on photography from the first half of the 20th century and, in addition, he had recently made a book of photographs with Halsman called *Dalí's Mustache*. Along with the photographic advice he also gave me some frankly surreal ideas. Interesting, all of them, but very difficult for me to put into practice, since they were terribly expensive to make. By way of example, I will explain a couple of them. One day he told me that I ought to take a picture of an exploding bull: that is, get a bull, fill it with explosives, throw it up in the air, make it explode and shoot the photo. Then I would become known all over the world as the photographer who made a bull explode. I told him that the idea was very attractive, but that the animal protection people would protest. 'Better, man, better,' he replied, and he grew more and more enthusiastic: '…and inside the bull you can put a pig, and inside the pig, a dog, and rabbits, and sparrows…' On another occasion he suggested that I make a curtain of rice and project a slide onto it and then take a photo of it. If I did this, each grain of rice would have a small part of the image. A really good idea that was difficult to implement, inspired by the decomposition of the atom. He was, quite honestly, a surprising man. One autumn, when he was saying goodbye before returning to New York, he asked me to find him a woman with a very big bottom. I thought he was joking, of course, but much to my surprise, when he returned the following summer, the first thing he said was to ask if I had found the woman with the very big bottom! Despite his eccentricities, which were playing to the gallery more than anything else, I have to admit in all fairness that he was a true genius and a very hard worker –like Miró. I met both of them more or less in the same period, in fact, but working with and for both of them at the same time was too much for me. Slowly but surely, then, I started to gravitate towards Miró, because he was always here while Dalí, on the other hand, never stopped coming and going. One of the last photos I took of him was during a dinner in Cadaqués, at a dealer's house, at which Duchamp was also present.

Hemingway

When I was working for the Ministry of Information and Tourism taking tourist photos, on several occasions I had to go to Pamplona, where I coincided with the American writer, who was very much in love with the city and its San Fermín festival. Although we never spoke or so much as shook hands, I took several photographs of him, and I know for a fact that he was well aware of who I was, because on various occasions when we saw one another, whether up close or from a distance, or simply passed on the street he used to wink at me. I am very satisfied with some of the photographs I took of him, especially one I shot in the Pamplona bullring that I took from inside the barrier, in which he seems to be looking straight at me, though in reality what he is looking at is the bull in the arena. By the way, in order to get inside the barrier, I had to go to the police to obtain a permit. As the policeman was filling out the document, he asked if I was a journalist, and I told him that I was taking photos for the Ministry's catalogue and posters. He then said: 'Well, then, let's put you down as an artistic photographer.' I regret now not having kept this kind of certificate or permit that classifies me as an object worthy of admiration.

Josep Lluís Sert

I knew Josep Lluís Sert, or rather I knew him by name. He was a friend of my father's, as they were both members of GATPAC, a group to which almost all the intellectual avant-garde of the time belonged. When the construction of the new Roca jewellers' shop on Passeig de Gràcia was completed, the inauguration featured an exhibition of photographs by Man Ray, about which my father wrote a review article. This was my first contact with Sert, who shortly after was driven into exile by the war. When he eventually returned, he mistook me for my father, and that made a huge impression on him because for him I really was Pere Català i Pic, his friend who had not aged. The fact is that I do look a lot like my father…

Over the next few years, I was in close contact with Sert, as I photographed many of his buildings: the Fondation Maeght, Miró's studio in Mallorca, the Miró Foundation in Barcelona… I even went so far as to make a book paying to tribute the 'photoscopes' that Prats made with the photographer Joaquim Gomis, which I think of as my particular personal tribute to the architect.

Sert told me an interesting story about the International Exposition in Paris in 1937. At that time, Spain exported mercury, and they wanted this material to be represented in some way at the Expo. Now, a fountain of mercury had been built in Seville in 1929, and the plan was to transport this fountain to the Spanish pavilion in Paris. The fountain arrived at the very last moment, but it was completely at odds with the pavilion that Sert had designed, and the desperate architect tried to find a Spanish sculptor who could make him another one. He looked for González, for Gargallo… but the artists had already gone back to Spain, their

work on the pavilion being completed. By chance, Alexander
Calder went to visit Sert one day and he decided to ask him,
but Calder objected that he was not Spanish. Sert agreed that this
was true, but added that for him, from that moment on, Calder was
Calderón de la Fuente. Calder accepted the commission and
completed it very quickly, and we now have this fountain at the
Miró Foundation in Barcelona.

Sert's contribution to modern architecture is of the greatest
importance. I photographed many of his buildings, but on none
did I work as much as I did at the Miró Foundation in Barcelona,
where I received so many impressions. One of them is that Sert
conceived the Foundation building as a medieval monastery, with
its cloister, cells and courtyards with trees. Miró's idea was to plant
an olive tree and a carob tree to recall the Camp de Tarragona,
which required the use of a crane, because they could not be
brought in through the door. Natural light enters the interior
indirectly through the skylights and creates a diffuse overhead
illumination. Sert designed the building thinking that it would later
be expanded, with the octagonal tower as its centre, repeating the
earlier construction in reverse.

I also recall the day they brought to the Foundation's
collection point two sculptures that had been seized as plunder.
One was Chillida's sculpture *Meeting Place*, which had been placed
on Paseo de la Castellana, in Madrid, until a Francoist mayor had
it removed. It was then installed in a privileged location at the
Foundation for a few years, in exile, until with the transition to
democracy it could be returned to its original place. The other
is a magnificent Calder that was on Barcelona's Avenida General
Goded (now Avinguda de Pau Casals) for a short time. However,
the local ratepayers complained that it was not to their liking,
and the City Council duly removed it to the Miró Foundation,
where it now welcomes visitors, a testament to the great friendship
between Sandy Calder and Joan.

VI.
A brief personal note

I must insert here a brief personal note about myself. Valerie was an English woman who was a good friend of mine for several years, whom I visited a few times in London. However, we were never a couple, as such, because I had resolved that until I had fully established my professional career, I would not get married. And I kept to that resolution, since I did not feel that I was sufficiently established until I was forty, the age at which I finally got married. It is interesting, perhaps, that my female friends were almost always foreigners. So much so that the woman I married, the mother of my two children, is Danish. I did not marry before that because the one thing that interested me profoundly and in which I wanted to excel and make a name for myself was photography. Of course, if you are to do this, you must be completely dedicated to your work and not do or even think about anything else. By way of example, a Swiss friend once suggested that we spend a fortnight together in Mallorca, and I told her that it was impossible. I did not have to explain myself to anyone, I worked for myself, and I made great demands of myself, and that is why I was neither willing nor able to allow any distractions. I was on my own and therefore I needed a great deal of self-discipline if I was to achieve my goal of being a great professional photographer. But none of this should make you think that I was a loner or that I did not like and need women. Of course I did, as we all do! When my need for a woman and for sex really became too strong to ignore, I would go to a brothel. I am one of those people who are quite convinced that it was a mistake to get rid of them, although now things are not quite the same as before. I went there as if I were going to the barber's. It was a necessity and that's all there is to it!

On the other hand, for all the great number of women friends I always had, I only had one really deep friendship, one great personal relationship. So it was that when I felt that I had thoroughly resolved my financial and professional situation, I decided to take the step. I have always considered myself a balanced person and acted as such. And I honestly think I did not waste the best years of my life, because I was doing what interested me above all else and what I loved most: photography. I have thrown myself into my work above all, and I do so even now, but that has never led me to neglect my family responsibilities when the time came. And I took this very seriously when I separated from my wife and in terms of having custody of my two children, who at the time of the separation were aged eight and ten. I wanted to keep them because, in my opinion, my wife was someone whose behaviour was rather chaotic and I felt that, if the children stayed with her, they would end up being chaotic too. So I told them that I would take care of them until they were of age —until they were eighteen years old (although at that time a person did not come of age until twenty-one). We went to live in Maresme, in Mataró; I would take them to school, and they would have lunch there, but every evening I made their dinner.

I did everything. Like a father and a mother. I never needed anyone to help me, because I had everything very well organised. When the elder of the two was sixteen, we decided to return to Barcelona —I had not given up my apartment— and from the age of eighteen, I told them they could do whatever they wanted. I had fulfilled my promise to them. Curiously, or perhaps not so curiously, they then decided that they wanted to go and live with their mother. I am quite convinced that they did so because with me they had to do everything, absolutely everything. I gave them freedom, but also the capacity to learn to do things for themselves. And the truth is that I am very satisfied with the results. As for my ex-wife, over the years we arrived at a cordial atmosphere, and

I must thank her for the interest and concern she has shown in resolving the health problems I have had in recent years.

I met my wife, Lilly, when she came to Barcelona to practice the Catalan she had learned at university in Denmark. Naturally, I told her to stay, because I would teach her. A normal attitude, that of a person in love. And the truth is that, by and large, that is how it was, and after a short time she had learned to speak fluently. During the first years of our married life we were in the habit of travelling to Denmark twice a year for the summer holidays and for Christmas, and I continued to do this after the separation, for the children's sake. Naturally, this allowed me to get to know the country well, but not its language. I don't know if I have mentioned this, but the fact is that I am a total and absolute no-no when it comes to languages. In effect, I am confined to my native Catalan and to Spanish. Our stays in Denmark were not usually spent in Copenhagen but rather at my in-laws' house in the countryside, in Jutland, a place where modernity did not exist. For example, there were no toilets, so for those needs we had to go out to the stable or cowshed (just like when I was a boy and we used to spend our summers on the farm); on the other hand, there was a television and the corresponding labour-saving equipment for milking the cows. In other words, for them, convenience and comfort were not for the more domestic matters but for what constituted their means of living or their modus vivendi.

The first time I went to Denmark was before we were married, and everyone gave me the relevant advice, especially with regard to warm clothes, because in that country, they told me, it was very cold. The reality was that I did not feel at all comfortable there. On the contrary, I was stiflingly hot all day long, since their heating systems are very well-equipped, so the houses are always at the right temperature from October until spring, when they shut it off. Beneath my in-laws' house there was a semi-basement, where a man who only task was to take care of the heating lived. In return, he had a warm roof over his head all through the winter. Oddly enough, my wife started to feel —and suffer from— the cold when she came to live in Barcelona.

I realised then that the great cities, those that have real economic and financial power, are almost all in places where a cold climate is a constant or characteristic, and the people that live there have to organise themselves, at work, in such a way as to combat the cold and the darkness. On the other hand, it is easy to realise that the cities where the climate is kind and the pleasant temperature is conducive to a more outdoor life have not developed so much. However, this observation or reflection aside, we continued to go to Denmark for regular visits, especially after our two children were born; and after Lilly and I had separated, I continued to take the children to their maternal grandparents' house, which meant that I could make my trips around the world. I remember that on one of these visits, as I was about to leave the children, the younger one, Andreu, asked me to buy him a toy gun. I had rather definite views about these things, and I didn't want him to have a gun, because I was not at all in favour of war toys. At the time of our next visit there was a good deal of controversy in Denmark about whether to ban the sale of pornography and also of war toys. The Danish government was opposed to banning either of those two things should be. In the matter of guns, they argued that the Second World War had clearly shown that the people who used their weapons indiscriminately were precisely the ones that had not been allowed to play at soldiers when they were children. The very next day I went to a toy shop and bought the boy a toy pistol, and he played with it like mad, all day long; When it was time for bed, he left it on a table, and I put it somewhere safe, expecting that he would ask me for it when he wanted it. And he never mentioned it again. So the Danish government's argument finally convinced me. They used a similar argument about pornography. And I subsequently saw here, in this country, that the argument was quite valid and sensible: at first people are curious about it, then normality makes people get used to it and what was a novelty for a while ends up losing its appeal; it no longer excites curiosity and comes to be accepted as normal for those who are interested in it, and that's all there is to it! Such things are basically just fads. In fact, this always happens when people are free to decide for themselves. Banning things tends to have the opposite effect from what it is intended to: in other words, prohibitions are worth transgressing.

VII.
Travel and photojournalism

Travelling around Spain

Not only do I have a great memory of my first trip, it was also
one of the jobs that has given me the greatest satisfaction. This
was in the fifties, when the publisher Lara asked me to illustrate a
book about the magnificent city of Cuenca (about which I knew
nothing, of course). The truth is that I was delighted to accept the
offer, because I was very eager to get out and get to know Spain.
In other words, I was very excited to set off on my travels! The
publisher gave me the text for which I was to supply the images.
The writer was González Ruano, and the book surprised me
on the very first page. It was dedicated to the then Minister of
Trade and Industry, whose name was Arburúa. Curious about the
dedication, I asked Sr. Lara if the minister was from Cuenca. He
replied that he was not, and that if he dedicated the book to him
it was so that the minister would give him a truck. A very valuable
vehicle at that time, with which, of course, you could do a nice
bit of business, since you could sell it for a lot of money. With this
anecdote, then, I commenced what was too be a constant in my
professional life: travelling around Spain. And thus resolved to carry
out this assignment that filled me with satisfaction, the first thing
I did was buy a Vespa scooter. I then set off for Cuenca and the
pending interview with the author of the text, González Ruano,
who explained to me the genesis of the book, a curious story that
is well worth sharing. In those years a Catalan, a certain Julià, was
the civil governor of the province, and this governor, González
Ruano told me, had been concerned that the city should be as well

supplied as the times (the height of the black market period) would
allow. More than that, he had even made it possible for the writer
to have a house on one of the most emblematic streets in the city,
Calle San Pedro. Indeed, it was not only González Ruano who
had been blessed with one of these houses; several other artists and
intellectuals were also beneficiaries and were duly grateful. That is
how González Ruano came to write the book dedicated to the
beautiful province of Cuenca, which I ended up knowing as well as
or even better than Barcelona. In Cuenca, then, I learned the best
and most profound lessons of my profession, which is to say that
I learned many things about photography on which I subsequently
expanded –and how!– when taking photographs all over Latin
America, where I also came to understand many things about Spain.

For example: in Cuenca there is a town called Villaescusa de
Aro, a very small town that is little more than a crossroads and,
according to González Ruano, fourteen bishops had been born
there –something I could not believe. It turns out, however, that
in that town they had built a collegiate church that served as a
seminary. The population of the town and the surrounding area
consisted almost entirely of farmers, whose brightest sons were sent
to the seminary and inevitably ended up becoming priests and,
years later, ended up in America, where they were needed. I saw
this clearly –it dawned on me– in Mexico, where I had gone to
do a book on traditional crafts with Sigfrid Blume. The town that
brought me to realise this was called Jesús María and was three days
journey from the valley of Tepic, the capital of the state of Nayarit.
In fact, however, it didn't take us that long to get there, as we ended
up going by plane. We landed in a cattle field and stayed in the
town for three or four days, living in huts, like everyone else there,
yet there was a cathedral in the town! The bishop must have been
from Villaescusa de Aro.

Now, before going to America, I was in Madrid, on account
of the work I was doing on the tourist routes of Spain. In Santa
Maria de la Huerta, a little town in Soria, there was a monastery
like the one in Poblet, surrounded by a wall about two kilometres

round which served to enclose an orchard and vegetable garden. This was certainly the practice ground of the corresponding seminary where the trainee priests taught to work the land before being sent to the Americas. At least that is how I have interpreted the events I have been describing.

From all my travels I have learned that I was a great observer of people and things. Or perhaps I have learned so much because I have always been a great observer.

One of the greatest and most emotional experiences in all my work as a photographer was the arrival in Barcelona of the *Semiramis*, the ship on which the fighters of the Blue Division returned to Spain after years in prisoner-of-war camps. At the time I was working for the weekly magazine *Revista* and of course I was commissioned to do a photo report on the enormous expectation that had been created around the ship and on the arrival in Barcelona of the numerous relatives of the repatriated Spaniards. I was one of the privileged few who were allowed to board the ship with the pilot in charge of the docking manoeuvre. This is why many of my photographs capture the faces and emotion of the relatives from the point of view of the former prisoners. They are photos of an absolute realism.

In the 1950s, when the Ministry of Information and Tourism hired me to do photo reports from all over Spain (on tourism, of course), I was in contact with the director-general of the Ministry, but the person I dealt with in person was Salvador Pons, who was very pleasant and efficient (there was always someone that was). In fact, this contact with the Ministry came about by chance. When I started on my own, away from my father, I had not much work, since it was not so easy to establish a clientele when the only clients I knew were my father's, whom I could not take away from him. One of the first things I did was a series of large-format screens, which were exhibited in Sala Gaspar. A very good idea, but unfortunately they were not much of a commercial success. Some little time after the screen exhibition, a printer named Riuset told me that people in Madrid were trying to contact me, but as they did not have my address and I did not have a telephone number they did not know how to find me. So, without any hesitation, I went to Madrid. The people looking for me were the architects Corrales and Molezún, who had been commissioned by the Government to design the Spanish Pavilion for the World's Fair in Brussels and wanted me to take some large-format photos for the pavilion. It was evident that they had seen the exhibition of screens in Sala Gaspar and had liked my project. This made me see that when someone has a good idea and knows how to work with it and make it happen, in the long run it ends up yielding good results. I never sold any of those screens, but they gained me this magnificent opportunity.

Also involved in this story was Salvador Pons, who was in charge of the campaign to promote tourism and the planning of my trips around Spain. Some curious anecdotes from that time are now part of its graphic history, because, whatever I was told to do, I always tried to do more. For example, during Holy Week in Seville, it was impressed on me that what I should photograph above all were the religious images such as the Macarena, the people in the processions, the candles, the *saeta* singers, the men carrying the floats and the expressions of devotion on the faces of the onlookers. At the same time, I was never to photograph the pointed hoods, because they could give a bad impression to foreigners (I suppose because they were so much like the Ku Klux Klan). I fulfilled my contractual obligation, of course, but my sense of professional duty demanded that I capture other images of Holy Week in Seville; the Holy Week that is today a constituent part of the history of Spain in those years. I photographed everything and everyone: the men in hoods, the priests, the girls —pretty or ugly, young of old. I was thinking, precisely, about the future, about photographic history.

On another of my trips I had to go to Valencia to do a photo report on the *fallas*. The newly made *fallas* in all their grandeur and spectacle. However, I took the opportunity to take a different kind of photo, shot from inside the shell of the *fallas*, to capture the faces of the people who had come to see them. I also wanted to photograph the fireworks, and I even tried to take a photo of the *mascletà* pyrotechnics; I say tried, because when everything started to explode I found it impossible to shoot a single photo, since everything was moving under my feet!

Another important report was one about the Camino de Santiago pilgrimage route. The first time I went, I shot it in black and white. They then asked me to do another one and shoot some of it in colour. Now, I could not do that, because my particular mentality will not allow me to do such a thing, alternating the two systems, so I was obliged to do the route twice more. I did it on the Vespa along all but deserted roads only alleviated by the occasional appearance of a cart pulled by oxen or women carrying packages balanced on their heads. Every now and then, very rarely, a car would pass, usually with a Barcelona license plate, and when the driver saw my Barcelona license plate, they would honk the horn in greeting. In addition to this Camino de Santiago, what I remember from Galicia are two valleys on either side of a hill. Once a year a fair was held at the top, which allowed the inhabitants of the two valleys to meet again. (I experienced this again years later in Guatemala, in a Mayan village called Chichicatenagua.) Naturally, the people of the valleys wore their traditional costume, and one thing that caught my curiosity was that all the women were dressed in black, because every time a male relative died, they had to go into mourning for two years. And usually another one would die before the first mourning was over, so that was why they were permanently dressed in black.

I witnessed a similar celebration shortly after the end of World War II, in the Roncal valley in Navarre, where the people of the valleys of Navarre in Spain and France gathered at the top of the Pierre de Saint Martin, because every three years the inhabitants of one valley had to give three cows to the inhabitants of the other in return for the right of pasture. I had been asked to report on it, and I remember that we spent the night in Isaba, the capital of the Roncal valley. I set out at midnight, with the mayor and six other dignitaries; we were on horseback and accompanied

by a dozen others on foot. At eight in the morning we arrived
at a spring where a group that had started before us had already
prepared breakfast for us. From there we continued the journey
to the summit, right on the border between the two valleys of the
Navarrese and French Pyrenees. There were already a lot of people
there from the French side, because there was a road that enabled
them to reach the summit with ease. Most of the people who
arrived from France were Spanish refugees who had come to the
celebration to meet their relatives who were also taking advantage
of the fair. The ritual began with all the authorities, on both sides,
placing their hands on the stone. The last to do so was the mayor
of Isaba. After that, the French brought twelve cows, of which the
people of Roncal chose the three best, and then six more, because
in the previous two years it had not been possible to perform the
ritual because the Germans had closed the border. Then there was
a big lunch and a big party. We returned to Isaba at night, and on
the way back the cows were sold to the people from Roncal who
wanted to buy them.

When I was working on the book about Cuenca, I heard
about a bullfight that was to be held one Sunday in the little
town of Carrascosa del Campo. I made a point of going there to
take some photos of the bullfight and of the excavation of some
Roman remains being carried out there. I spoke to Florencio
Cañas, Cuenca City Council's spokesman for culture, and he told
me that if I needed anything or had any problems, I should contact
his colleague in Carrascosa del Campo, because they were old
acquaintances. I went there in the morning, and I was early enough
to find the people of the town setting up the bullring in the square
with their carts.

I went to the town hall to talk to the councillor responsible
for culture and explain what I wanted to do. He accompanied me
to the square to see that I got a good spot, and I noticed that the
flags they were putting up were those of the so-called Axis powers:
Spain, Italy, Japan and Germany. Naturally, I asked if they were not
concerned that some American (there were already quite a few

in Spain) should see them and be very disturbed that the streets
and the square were decked with swastikas. The councillor, poor
fellow, asked me what a swastika was. I pointed to the flag and he
replied that he would speak to the mayor. To make the most of
my time there I then went to take some photos in Salóbrica and
Valeria, the two neighbouring villages where they were excavating
Roman archaeological remains. When I returned to Carrascosa del
Campo in the afternoon for the bullfight, I found that they had
taken down all the flags. I was able to do an exceptional report,
which would nowadays be published in all the gossip magazines,
because the bullfight was organised by the toreador Dominguín,
who had an estate just outside the town. Dominguín had staged
this *corrida* to impress his fiancée, Lucía Bosé, and Domingo Ortega
and Antonio Bienvenida accompanied him in the bullring. What a
great bill for a small town! More or less from that time on I have
kept many celebratory articles (which I appreciate for all that they
mean) about different aspects of my work as a photographer. I
like them all, needless to say, for their flattery, but for this chapter I
thought it appropriate to reproduce some short excerpts. The first
of these, entitled 'Dizziness', is by César González Ruano and was
published in 1955, in *ABC* or *Arriba*, I don't remember which. It
goes like this:

*It so happened that in these last few days the photographer Català
Roca [sic] came to Cuenca to take photographs for a guide to the province
that I am preparing. And this most agreeable man and excellent professional
set himself, morning and afternoon, to carrying out his task, which at times
was not easy. Català Roca went up to the Castle at the top of the town
followed by a most respectful group of children who were eager to afford
possible assistance as well as to earn a penny. From time to time, they broke
through his wall of silence with some offer of optical service:*
   –Would you like me to show you the castle?
   –Shall I accompany you to see the cemetery?
   *On the bank of the Júcar river in the clear afternoon, on top of
the great rocks, our photographer climbed up on some advanced stones
overlooking the deep abyss.*

—Be careful not to fall.

—Don't be careful.

And then a little boy who could not have been more than seven years old said to another, out of who knows what labyrinths of thought and reasoning, this wonderful and disconcerting phrase:

—You tell him to get down, because rich people get dizzy easily.

This warning made me laugh and gave me much to think about. 'Rich people get dizzy easily.'… I don't believe Català Roca is very rich, but that is not the point. He was dressed like a tourist, like a man who lives in a hotel, who can naturally take a taxi and go into a café whenever he wishes. In short, a rich man, in the boy's eyes. And a rich man whom the boy judged to be unaccustomed to a hard life, to risk, to vertigo.

The other excerpt is from the magazine *El Ruedo. Semanario gráfico de los toros*, number 962, 29 November 1962. In this article, commenting on the book *Tauromaquia* by Néstor Luján, the author dedicates a short section to photo-bullfighting. It goes like this:

AN INCIDENT. PHOTO BULLFIGHTING.

And now we shall set aside for a moment our review of the literary work to enter the graphic domain of F. Català Roca [sic], who presents a series of documents sensational not only for their artistic value but also for having discovered a means of placing modern photographic technique in the service of a current concept of bullfighting. We are not referring to the numerous photos, which are a true artistic compendium, but to those other inspirations in what the Saxon foreigners call 'dynamic photos' and in which both the static and the mobile bodies are captured with an Einsteinian sense of relativity.

In the ordinary snapshot, in the work of bullfight photographers until now, the only concern has been to capture —with all the actors immobilised— the centre or culmination of the suerte *manoeuvres from the most favourable angle of framing. In this way the* torero *is glamourised and beautiful photos may be obtained for the posters; to the point that the great aspiration of poster artists today is to paint posters as exact and as devoid of imagination as the photos.*

F. Català Roca matches the rhythm of his shutter to the original conception of his Tauromachy. With full figures —those of the bullfighter—

*and blurred silhouettes —those of the bull— he invents 'photo-bullfighting',
a new and surprising way of criticising the* suertes *and appraising
their truth.*

The verónica, *the long* cambiada, *the* parón *with feet together
and the* ayudado por alto *are all the more legitimate —and the theory is
documented by the photos in this beautiful book— the longer the bullfighter
has stood motionless before the dynamic impact of the bull, which attacks
blindly and moves, leaving a fearful wake in the photographic emulsion of
the film.*

*F. Català Roca's technique has come to explode the aphorism that
even a bad manoeuvre will have an excellent photo. From now on we will
place our trust only in the graphic documents of 'photo-bullfighting'. It is
these that will prove or denounce, with the decisive study of the bullfighter's
profile, whether he remained still as the bull's horns tickled his femoral
nerve.*

*The photographic work of F. Català Roca is not only illustration and
complement, but invention and substance in this sumptuous Tauromachy.*

This article, signed by a certain Don Antonio, has
strengthened my resolve to never lower the bar, to never let myself
be carried away by fads and fashions, to always do what I consider
to be right for photography. It is just as bad to know too little
as to know too much, on any subject, and whenever I find myself
disagreeing with editors, graphic designers, promoters, curators,
conservators and the like in the world of photography, I always
think of the ordinary person who knows how to rightly value
work well done with simplicity and honesty. Thank you, Don
Antonio; thank you.

Travelling in the Americas

As for my trips to America, they were occasioned by Blume's
decision to publish a series of books on the traditional popular
crafts of various countries in South and Central America, including
Mexico, which was the first one I worked on, and led to the series
being continued with other American craft traditions. It goes
without saying that they had no need to twist my arm, because this

commission promised a double pleasure: that of travelling, which I
have always loved, and taking photos, which is what I enjoy most
in the world. However, I had to do these reports in parts, since I
had recently separated from my wife and I was in sole charge of
my two children, who were still very young. I had to combine the
work with the children, so during the school term I was there for
them, and during the school holidays I took them to their maternal
grandparents in Denmark and was able to go to America.

The countries that I liked best, and in which I enjoyed taking
photographs the most, were Mexico and Guatemala; and Peru
and Bolivia for the ancient civilisations of the Mayans and Aztecs
[*sic*]. I was in Chile shortly after General Pinochet became head
of state. I realised that, compared to the other countries of South
America, Chile was one of the most developed. I think that this
was essentially due to a large German population, loaded with
money, who were most certainly the people who supported
Pinochet and financed him, and as such, in my view, are jointly
responsible for the killing of President Allende. In fact, they are
still a very important group. I remember that during my stay they
were staging some kind of German festival which their European
relatives were visiting, because they could not return. The cantata
Carmina Burana by Carl Orff, a notorious Hitlerite, was being
performed. At the same time, I also believe that the US protected
the Pinochet coup d'état and actively supported it, because it
furthered the anti-communist policy so dear to the Americans.
The impression I formed of Brazil is that sooner or later it would
become one of the strongest and most important countries on
the continent.

However, as I have already said before, the fact is that, in
every way, the most interesting parts of my trips to the Americas to
photograph the wealth of indigenous craftsmanship were Mexico,
Guatemala and Canada. In Canada I even went to the Arctic. There
I recalled what my father had told me on several occasions about
the filmmaker Robert Flaherty, who had made a docudrama about
an Eskimo, entitled *Nanook of the North*. I remember seeing it when

I was very young, at the Borràs cinema. Flaherty shot this film with a special orthochromatic stock (which is not sensitive to the colour red, so it can be developed without having to be completely in the dark). This is exactly what came to my mind when I was on Baffin Island with Marta Ribalta, who was working for the Blume publishing house at the time. We went there by plane and when we were due to return we found there were no flights for another fifteen days. We were fortunate that a medical case had to be urgently evacuated, and we were able to take advantage of the emergency flight. Honestly, despite the spectacular nature of the landscape, we didn't like the place much; I realised that the Eskimos were very marginalised and marginal and at the same time very rude. And the crafts they made were a mockery, fake, in that they did indeed make leather goods by hand, but only and exclusively for sale.

At the same time, returning now to the United States, the crafts they make there must be considered not as popular and traditional but as a type of handiwork learned in school and made from the most commonplace materials: fabrics, wood, ceramics… I went as far as the capital of Tennessee, Nashville, where I found that their craft products are marked by a very strong European influence. There, I came across a little shop with the name of a Catalan girl: her parents were from Lloret de Mar.

New York

I have to acknowledge that no other city or country has impressed me as much as New York. It is completely different from any other city in the world. I have never really got to know Rome, for example, but I feel as if I had been there or known it all my life; I have seen photographs that have shown me what it is like and what its landscapes and architecture are like. A landscape, an architecture and a culture, indeed, very close to my own. New York is something else entirely —a true spectacle!

The first two or three times I went to New York, I was only there for a few hours, on a stopover on my way to Canada, but

although I saw almost nothing, I could already sense that it was
one of the cities I would end up liking most. Some years later,
I went there because the Institute of North American Studies
in Barcelona arranged for an exhibition of my photographs, in
February 1987. On that visit I had little time to walk around, but
fortunately, the following September, I had the opportunity to
go back and had enough time to get to know the city and take a
whole pile of photographs. On that occasion I became aware of
what a fascinating, enchanting city New York is and I discovered a
lot of interesting things there, so it ended up making a very strong
impression on me. It was on this particular stay that I suddenly
realised that one day I would make a book entirely of New York
photographs, without any text. Only the strength of the image,
which is what really struck me. As I have said, I do not speak any
foreign language, so I could not ask questions or inquire about
anything, and I basically took in New York through my eyes, so it is
my eyes that must explain it.

One of the many things that caught my attention was the
architecture of the city, and its enormous skyscrapers. In seeking
to get to know different aspects of the city, on each of my visits I
have stayed in different hotels in different areas of that great city. If
Paris is traditionally thought of as the city of light, New York is, in
my modest opinion, undoubtedly the city of reflections, and, what
is more, of misogyny. I have written somewhere that Barcelona is
the city of women, on account of the great number of sculptures
of women to be seen in its architecture, and New York is entirely
the opposite. I have never seen a single sculpture of a woman there;
all of those I have seen are of men and very different from the
sculpted figures here. They are mostly of seated men wearing
coats and hats, quite the opposite of what we see here, where the
figure is standing, or on horseback, and so many statues are of
military men. The ones in New York are sculptures or monuments
dedicated to ordinary, normal characters from civil society, as they
are now called: bankers, businessmen, artists… Although I said
that I had not seen any statues or sculptures of women, I must

correct that by saying that I saw some at the Rockefeller Centre, but of course, where there are images of women it is in the British, French and Italian pavilions. The Americans have nothing, they only have the Statue of Liberty and what's more it is outside the city, on a little island… Because they haven't let her come in!

New York is also a city full of photographs… I mean, it is a city that offers you an immense possibility of capturing many and varied moments. For example, I really enjoyed spending a lot of time in Central Park just watching people go by. I would buy a bag of nuts, and the squirrels would come right up to me until someone appeared with a dog and then they would run away.

At the same time, the mix of races is another of the city's attractions. In Chinatown everything is Chinese, in Little Italy, which is becoming less and less Italian and more Asian, everything is Italian… The Jewish quarter, especially 47th Street with its typical and traditional jewellers, or rather, jewellery stores, is known as the heart of the diamond district. In New York, absolutely everything is a spectacle. That is why it is the city I have photographed the most after Barcelona. I must say, however, that despite being fascinated by New York, I would not like to live there for very long. I find it too mechanised, too full of offices…

Central Park has always made me think of our Ciutadella park; at bottom, they both seem to me to rather like cemeteries, due to the great number of statues and monuments in each commemorating people who have been dead for a good many years. One of the ones I remember from Central Park is of the Cuban revolutionary José Martí, and another is dedicated to the battleship USS *Maine*, which exploded and sank, thereby sparking the war between Spain and the United States.

SoHo is another neighbourhood that is well worth a visit, thanks to the number of art galleries there, like in the Born district of Barcelona. One of the things that I took a long time to discover in New York was the subway, which I had never used until my son Martí accompanied me on one of my last trips. I usually travelled with my editor or with Marta Ribalta, who was

the person entrusted with making the contacts I needed to be able
to take the photos I was interested in taking. On those last few
trips, which I only took for the pure pleasure of photographing
the city at my own pace, I went with my son, who managed to
persuade me see that it was much better to travel around the city
by subway rather than by taxi, as I had been in the habit of doing.
One very effective means of capturing new images, which I did
very discreetly, was to use the small camera that I always carry with
me. Another interesting thing that I discovered is what I think of
street archaeology: everywhere I went I noticed traces of the old
rail tracks that must have been laid all over the city. However, what
I found most curious is that, in many places, these tracks must have
run through what were now apartment buildings, and instead of
lifting the rails they had simply asphalted on top of them! By the
way, I have a photograph of a sidewalk in which the impression
of a leaf from a tree is clearly visible. It must be that when they
had just poured the tarmac and it was not yet completely dry, the
leaf fell and remained there, framed as if it were a painting. Very
near Washington Square, there is a monument by Picasso, made
with the same technique as the one on the Col·legi d'Arquitectes
building in Barcelona. And in the Rockefeller Center, as everyone
knows, there are some murals by Sert, which, I am sorry to say, I
found very disappointing. The fact is that, compared to those in
the Saló de les Cròniques in Barcelona City Council and in Vic
Cathedral, the murals in New York are very weak and excessively
monumental; but, of course, that is what Americans like.

The city of New York was built thanks to the conjunction of
three elements, namely stone, iron, and electricity.

The centre of New York is the island of Manhattan, a great
rock that sticks up from the Hudson River, a good solid base
capable of supporting the weight of the skyscrapers.

Iron is an element that has accompanied humanity since
ancient times, when it was used to make tools and weapons,
but it was not until the end of the nineteenth century that
the extraordinary versatility of this material when applied to

construction was discovered. The Eiffel Tower in Paris is one of
the first iron constructions, created precisely to demonstrate the
possibilities of this new use of an age-old material. So it was that
by piling up iron beams on the rock, very tall buildings could be
erected; but who would live up there having to go up and down
countless stairs? Who would go down every day to get a loaf of
bread or whatever? Thanks to electricity, these and other problems
were able to be solved. Elevators would transport people, and
pumps would take water up to the roof to fill the wooden tanks,
many of these wooden tanks can still be seen today.

Barcelona

Some of my most vivid memories of Barcelona, a city of which I
am not a native but I love just the same, date from when my family
decided to move there. I was nine years old at the time, and those
memories are focused on the Ciutat Vella district, since we lived on
Carrer del Pi and I went to the Condal school, which is located
next to the Palau de la Música. In any case, my most important
memories of these early years are focused almost exclusively on
La Rambla, which was where we used to go to meet our friends
and fellow pupils, some of whom also lived very close to Plaça
Nova… Pere Ardanuy, Mas, and others, lived there. The outer edges
of Barcelona were Poble Sec, Poblenou and Gràcia, places that we
did not know because we did not move out of the centre where
we lived. A practical joke we used to play from time to time was to
go to La Rambla on a Sunday afternoon, when everyone used
to go there to stroll up and down. We would form a line, ten or
twelve abreast, and take up practically the whole avenue, not letting
anyone pass us and walking slowly until there was open space in
front of us and thronged with people behind us. One of the few
occasions when I would leave the city centre was to go to Horta,
by tram of course, to see some relatives. That was when I saw the
Sagrada Família for the first time. I got to know the Eixample
because my father taught at the Escola Industrial there, when the
Eixample largely consisted of vacant lots. Tradition has it that on

the right side of the Eixample, from Carrer de Balmes to Passeig de Sant Joan, was where the upper class, the wealthiest people lived. And from Balmes to Plaça d'Espanya, that is, the left side, lived those who did not have so much money, although, to judge by some of the buildings, that did not seem to be the case. Over the years, Barcelona and I myself have experienced other Eixamples.

I have sometimes been asked if, after travelling so much all around the world, Barcelona seems to me one of the best cities. Of course, although I have travelled a lot, I have only seen a tenth of it… Moreover, it is difficult for me to answer this question because, in reality, to know is to love, and the longer you live in a city, the more you love it. When I was young, I often thought that I was bound to end up living abroad. However, when I reached my thirties, I came to see that such a thing was impossible because every time I went away I realised that Barcelona was my home. It really was. And no matter how much I came to know another city, such as Madrid, which I got to know very, very well thanks to Juan Antonio Cabezas, for whose book on Madrid I took the photos, Barcelona was always very much Barcelona. And you learn to see and notice differences, although, in this case (concerning these two cities) the differences are, let's say, under the skin, differences of feeling. For example, in Barcelona I sense an architectural anarchy that –although years ago I was dead against it– I really like now, especially that of the Eixample. And in the Eixample, to give even more specific examples, what I like most are the trees, an element that breaks the monotony. If it were not for the trees, on many occasions the architecture of the Eixample would crush you. The most significant aspect of the presence of trees is the aesthetic changes produced by the changes of weather and season that transform the way the neighbourhood looks throughout the year. As for Madrid, there is an element that has become a key reference for me and that is the zarzuela. These works are, in fact, authentic portraits of the city, especially *La Revoltosa* and *La verbena de la Paloma*, to mention just two. This is in contrast to Barcelona, where my references are none other than my own life. Because wherever

I go in the city there is some part of my existence, personal or professional.

Also with regard to Barcelona, I agree with my good and much admired friend Lluís Permanyer that one of the crucial axes is Passeig de Gràcia. Whenever I am in some other big city –New York, for example– I miss Passeig de Gràcia and La Rambla. And on La Rambla, the Boqueria market. A unique and wonderful place that gives unparalleled pleasure by way of its fruit stalls, like a still life painted by one of the most brilliant artists. I love to walk through the Boqueria. However, speaking of La Rambla, I must mention here my feeling that there are some elements that have distorted it most notably. And those elements are none other than the flower stalls, bird fanciers kiosks and news stands, which contribute more than anything to constricting and saturating it, so that you cannot walk there in comfort. But what can we do about it? I have some good photographs of La Rambla from the old days.

That said, I am not at all nostalgic for the past; on the contrary, I feel optimistic because I can see that the things that have changed over the years have improved the lives of the city's people. For instance, this recent expansion that has emerged as a consequence of the new Vila Olímpica, which has enabled us to recover an area of the city that had been lost to us for many, many years. In light of this, I remember Artigas, who was born and raised on Carrer de la Cadena, telling me that he saw the sea for the first time when he was fourteen. In my own case, I remember that we would occasionally go there to swim, although we did not go very often. As I am referring to this recent expansion, it is worth recalling that one of the elements that allowed the city to expand beyond its old walls was the relocation of the cemeteries on Carrer dels Lledó and the Fossar de les Moreres, and also the opening of the Ciutadella park and Carrer de Ferran and Carrer de la Princesa… important streets until the city opened upwards with the Eixample.

Of all these various changes and events that explain aspects of the history of the city, a few have remained deeply engraved in my memory. For example, in the apse of the cathedral there are marks in the stone from the time when a market was held there, and the butchers would sharpen their knives on the wall. Not far away, in El Call, you can clearly see how the Jewish community that had lived there was organised. It has always been a remarkable neighbourhood, with its dairies, its jewellers, and the Can Jorba department store, which subsequently moved to Portal de l'Àngel. All the great beginnings moved to different neighbourhoods as the city grew. The Roca jeweller's, before it opened on Gran Via, was originally on La Rambla, near Plaça Reial. On Carrer Nou, I recall, there was a bar that I had often heard mentioned but until I went there for the first time, I didn't really understand the name: people called it Trincall, but in fact the signboard read Drink Hall in English. On the same street there was also Ca l'Emília, a well-known brothel of the highest class, which I visited several times as what was called a wallflower, that is, to look at the girls, who, due to the influence of the nearby Liceu, were very splendidly dressed.

Plaça del Pedró, where Carrer de l'Hospital and Carrer del Carme converge, or separate, is another of these places with historic charm. It was here that travellers coming from the south, from Valencia or Tarragona, arrived in Barcelona, and on reaching the square, they could choose whether to enter the city through the Boqueria market or by way of Porta Ferrissa. It was, in fact, the point of entry. Another of the places where I have seen a great change in recent years is Carrer de la Canuda, a sad and gloomy street bounded by a convent, which has since given way to Plaça Vila de Madrid. Carrer dels Tallers was always a little livelier, although it was very closed-in, because what is now Plaça de Castilla did not exist then. There had been an old hospital there, the Military Hospital, and the church that still stands was part of the hospital complex.

I have always walked around the city a lot, which is why I have all these memories of it that have become this series of impressions. One of the things that I still want to do is put together a book of photographs I would like to call *La pell de Barcelona*, 'the skin of Barcelona', which would show the passage of time through

the façades of the city. I have a whole stack of photographs,
including one that was awarded the Ciutat de Barcelona prize and
was featured on the front page of *La Vanguardia*. I took it in front
of the Palau de Justícia, where there were two elaborate mosaics.
When they remodelled the area, these mosaics disappeared, and
all the time and money that must have gone into were forgotten.
Another of these photographs is of an old *masia* farmhouse on
Plaça de Lesseps, which was demolished shortly after the square
was laid out. I also remember that where the Dr. Fleming gardens
are now, there had been a building on a chamfered corner with a
full-height painted sign that read 'Clínica española. Colocación de
nodrizas' (Spanish clinic. Placement of wet nurses). All that survives
now of these and other places all over the city that has undergone
so many changes are my photographs. I would also like to do a
book about the architectural anarchy of Barcelona; an anarchy
brought about by a competitive impulse to score points but which
now, with the passage of time, has come to have a certain charm.
This fondness I have for anarchy, at least for visual anarchy, must
be due to my being a product of rural Tarragona, where it can be
seen above all in the trees. In contrast to the Empordà, with its
tall slender cypress trees, regularly spaced, Tarragona has a twisted
landscape of carob and almond trees… It is an anarchy made,
however, through an order. The trees were planted in an orderly
manner, but then they grew just as they wanted. I am a bit like that.
I like order, method, but I am also a bit anarchic, although without
descending into total anarchy.

I have mentioned the first time I saw the Sagrada Família,
but I want to return to the subject because, while I consider
Gaudí an architectural genius, I also believe that his work, now so
monumental and important, has no other reason for existing than
in the service of the wealthy and powerful. Because the buildings
that Gaudí designed could only be lived in by people with a lot
of domestic servants. Gaudí was almost a contemporary of Mies
van der Rohe, but in my opinion he was out of date and incapable
of looking to the future, both in his conception of space and in

the materials he used. Although I regard the Sagrada Família as
a symbol of Barcelona and believe that it should be finished, I
also believe that this should not be done the way they are doing
it. First and foremost, because it no longer makes much sense to
build a temple of this nature. The great temples of the present
age are the football stadiums. I believe that an architect such as
Sert or Coderch should have continued the Sagrada Família.
And as for the sculptures by Subirachs, I think that, despite the
criticisms, they will always be an improvement on the human
figures that Gaudí placed on the Nativity façade, where what I
like best is the wealth of organic forms and zodiacal symbols that
cover it. Gaudí really did have a global vision of the work, while
Subirachs gives the sculptures an excessive prominence; they are
too visible, an eyesore that detracts from Gaudí's work as a whole.
And let me be clear that I am not against Gaudí as such, because
La Pedrera seems to me to be a splendid building, albeit not very
practical. In contrast, Mies van der Rohe was the very opposite
of Gaudí; he was simplicity personified, although I am convinced
that there are still many people who do not understand him. His
Barcelona Pavilion is an eloquent example of this. I would like
to do a comparative study of Mies van der Rohe and Gaudí. And
speaking of books, another one well worth doing could be called
Barcelonines, 'Barcelona women', since you only have to look up
to realise how many female figures there are on our buildings.
The city is full of them! I know many places all over the world,
but I have never found one with as many figures of women on its
façades as Barcelona.

VII.
Meditations

Point of view

I am referring not to a point of view on a specific issue, but to point of view understood as the optical vision we have of things. To explain what I mean, let me say that most of us have two points of view, because we have two eyes. This allows us to see things in relief. A boy who was two metres tall once told me that when he entered a house, often the first thing he would see were the newspapers that the ladies put on top of the cupboards to collect dust. A person who was only one and a half metres tall could not have seen this, but on the other hand they would have a much better view of the keyholes. When I left Valls, I was nine years old and one metre tall, so I naturally had a very different idea of distances and heights than I had when I grew to one and a half metres. Distances seemed shorter to me. This different vision or point of view figures in an anecdote from the 11 September commemoration in 1932. I was at the monument to Rafael Casanova with my father when President Francesc Macià arrived. He was a very tall man, and I was right beside him, and as I was so small, my eyes were level with his hands. I was struck by the fact that he was holding a cabbage leaf in one hand, and did not let go it throughout his speech. But of course it was not a cabbage leaf, as I later realised: what the president was holding was a leaf or a sprig from the wreath he had just laid in front of the monument.

Regarding the framing of a portrait photo, in most cases it is vertical, when in fact it would be more logical for it to be landscape, due to the natural fact that our eyes are next to each other and not one on top of the other. Why, then, are most of these images in the upright format? My theory is that this comes from the invention of writing. The lines could not be too long because when you reached the end of a line you had to be able to see the start of the next; but you would also see the start of the first line, so you had to decide which was the right one to continue reading normally. To make reading easier, then, the text is set in two columns. Another way in which we are totally deformed —or formed, depending on how you look at it— is the scale of the photo (in relation to reality). I remember taking a photo of some sparrows in a tree on La Rambla. It was night, and the scene was like Japanese lacquerware. I enlarged the print to a metre and a half to make a folding screen and the little birds looked like partridges! They were too big. But if I had made them smaller they would still have looked like sparrows. We are more accustomed to seeing things reduced than enlarged. On another occasion, I took a photo that was a close-up detail of a partridge, and when I enlarged it to five times the size it looked like a fragment of a tapestry and not a partridge, thanks to the manipulation of the photographic scale.

Architecture

In this book you will find a plate which was an attempt to make a portrait of six architects, not by representing their faces but by selecting an image that reflected the personality of each one through one of their works.

The first is a house in Madrid by Coderch. The shadows cast on the white walls by the trees produce a continuous change in the decoration.

The second is a detail of the main door of the Fundació Joan Miró, by Josep Lluís Sert. I liked the play of light on the reinforced concrete of the arcades so much that I suggested this photo for the cover of a book that I illustrated, but the publishers did not understand it and rejected it.

The third is the Plaza de los Fueros in Vitoria, by Luis Peña Ganchegui in collaboration with the sculptor Eduardo Chillida, where the light does so much to define the sinuous layout of the seating in the amphitheatre.

The fourth is the staircase of the Mútua Metal·lúrgica in Barcelona, by Josep Martorell and Oriol Bohigas, which reminds me of a mechanical saw or a cogwheel.

The fifth is by Antoni de Moragas i Gallissà. The skillful arrangement of the bricks in the lobby of a block of flats creates very suggestive shapes. For some years now I have been thinking it would be worth doing a book showing how something as simple as a humble brick can give rise to a great wealth and variety of forms.

The sixth and last is by Francisco Juan Barba Corsini and consists of a conversion of the attic spaces of La Pedrera, where the laundry rooms and the servants' quarters had been, to create luxury flats. It is worth noting that before the lifts were installed, the upper floors were not much appreciated. In a sense, then, Barba Corsini can be said to have concluded this work of Gaudí.

I now think that, rather than a portrait of the architects by way of their works, what I have done is photograph their calligraphy.

Very personal opinions

Ever since I was a child, and therefore since my first years in Valls, I have associated the sanctuary of Lourdes with neo-Gothic architecture, and this must surely be due to a convent in that style, the Cor de Maria, in Valls. I had also seen photographs of Lourdes, and I connected the two because they were similar. Frankly, I came to dislike the style quite strongly. Later, I heard about another sanctuary, that of Fátima, and the miracles that were said to have taken place there. I am not a declared and inflexible anticlerical, but these two places produce a certain repulsion in me, although I have never been to either.

Once, during a stay in Lisbon to take some photos of the paintings by Maria Helena Vieira da Silva in the Fundação Calouste Gulbenkian, I observed a group of schoolchildren as they entered the museum; they did so in such a way, silently, and with such respect, as if it were a church or a shrine. Their behaviour set me to thinking that churches were, in effect, being replaced by art galleries. Thus, the Louvre would become the new Lourdes and the Gulbenkian the new Fátima.

As for my relationship with animals, I must say that I do not consider myself their enemy, but neither am I very much their friend; at any rate, I do not like having them around. My first real contact with animals was during the summers we spent at the *masia* near Valls. Of course, like any small child, I played with lizards and grasshoppers, because I considered them to be cute little creatures and not at all dangerous. But others bothered me a lot, such as mosquitoes, which I systematically dedicated myself to burning with a candle every evening before I went to bed. Poor mosquitoes!

When I was a little older and we were living on Avinguda del Tibidabo, I remember my contribution to the move was to ensure the safe arrival of the canary we had at that time, which I carried on foot to our new home. To conclude, my final relationship with animals dates from the post-war years. At Ca l'Estevet I met a young foreign woman who was going back to her own country for a while. She had a little fish and asked me if I would look after it when she was away. I was living in the residence on Carrer de Musitu at the time, and I said yes, so she brought me the fish with its food and the appropriate instructions. As I wanted to do my best for it, on Sundays I would fill the bath and put the little fish in the water so that it could swim to its heart's content. We became such great friends that I even gave it a name: Lopez, a combination of *lo* –'the'– and *pez* –'fish'.

With the perspective of the years we see things differently. As age, you think, reflect and compare the different situations in which you may find yourself or have found yourself throughout your life. To make a comparison with photography, we could say that when you are young you see things from a flat perspective, and when you get older you see everything in relief. On that premise I have also reflected on various aspects of life that I have seen and been affected by. These are simply things that I think, right or wrong, but they express my feelings and my way of thinking. Just after the war, I was in a camp in Santa Fe del Montseny with a group of hikers, there to climb Les Agudes, and when we started out, I found myself next to a very congenial older gentleman, Co de Triola, a friend of my father. As we walked the whole route together, he told me a great many things he had done in his life and particularly mentioned that he had been a great photography enthusiast, as a result of which he had founded the first company in Barcelona producing light-sensitive material. He was also a journalist and was one of the first to travel to Mallorca by plane. My curiosity was aroused, and I asked him what he was currently working on. He stopped in his tracks, looked at me and said: 'I have never worked!' I realised that without intending to, my question had offended him, since, belonging as he did to a wealthy family, had always done everything he for its own sake, for pure pleasure. In those days there were still people who believed that anyone who worked for a living was a contemptible or pitiful wretch.

At that time, too, only the rich had a car (I am thinking specifically of the pre-war period), and people used to say 'so-and-so is rich, because he has a car' as if it were a proven fact. A long time later, recalling this, it struck me that one of the reasons why Franco endured for so many years was that he made it possible for everyone —well, almost everyone— to have a SEAT 600. Another thing that has led me to reflect very deeply on all of this is the matter of envy. As the Catalan saying goes, if envy were ringworm, we would all be riddled with it. I remember, from long ago now, an enormous billboard in the Plaça de Gal·la Placídia, which bore the following legend or slogan: 'Dazzle your friends by buying a dream apartment.' In other words, the most important thing in life was to make yourself the envy of the people around you. As for cars, I hold to the theory that when they are simply a tool used only for work, they will cease to be an object of desire or a signifier of wealth. When this new and evidently somewhat utopian situation comes to pass, the stock phrase I cited above will change and we will say 'so-and-so is rich, because they don't have a car'. From this point of view, I can consider myself to be extremely rich because, as I have no need for a car, I don't have one!

I believe that the two world wars that have taken place in this twentieth century that is coming to an end are a single thing, in that they have been more like a drama in two acts: a first act from 1914 to 1918, and a second from 1939 to 1945. Hitler, in the second case, wanted to forge a united Europe dominated by Germany, which would become the lord and master of the world. That, in my opinion, is why there were so many so-called collaborators with the Hitler regime who believed in German hegemony in Europe. If my memory serves me, there were important collaborators in Norway, France, Belgium and even in Britain. The most important fact, or the most notable consequences of the two world wars, in my opinion, would be the apportioning of the continent based on the Potsdam agreements between the Allied powers and, ultimately, the fact that the world came to be divided between two great powers: the USSR, on the one hand, and the USA, on the other. In reality, the old form of colonisation by force of arms is gradually coming to an end (although this is actually very relative, because even now the world is never free of military conflict) and humanity is now being colonised in another way, perhaps more subtle but no less disturbing, in the form of colonisation by the dollar or the consumer society. Today, in fact, we are seeing how that division of the world between the USA and the USSR has gradually broken down with the disappearance or collapse of the communist Soviet bloc. Now, the world is faced with the fact that only one of the great powers —the USA— is the great coloniser, at least for a few long years.

I comment on these things because I lived through them when I was young and have gradually evaluated them and come to understand them as I have accumulated experience. I also think that many of these things are not explained to the younger generations or explained only in part and badly. I am one of those who believe that history is cyclical and repeats itself. I don't know if the schoolbooks explain that the Spain of Ferdinand VII and Napoleon's France, with shared political interests, joined forces against Portugal, but that alliance led to Spanish soldiers fighting on Napoleon's side in Denmark, much as, years later, in World War II, General Franco and Muñoz Grandes sent the Blue Division to fight for Hitler in the invasion of Russia. I learned about this when I went to Denmark and chanced to meet a butcher there with a very Spanish surname: Panduro. By the way, regarding the connection between Ferdinand VII and Napoleon, I should like to comment on the Spanish expression *hacer el primo*, 'to play the cousin', which is used of a gullible or naive person who is easily fooled or exploited. Apparently, this expression comes from the fact that Ferdinand VII used to start the letters he wrote to Napoleon with the greeting *Querido primo* –'Dear cousin'. And Ferdinand VII did indeed play the cousin.

Making a small leap ahead in time and historical events, I have always thought that Franco's dictatorship could not be toppled because the United States was perfectly happy with that regime, since it presented itself as a bulwark against the communism that threatened Western civilisation. And, undoubtedly, this was the reason that the famous Marshall Plan was considered unnecessary in Spain until many years later. The former Yugoslavia represents another small leap in distant but unfortunately current events. When the Germans invaded it, practically the whole population engaged in a guerrilla war against the Nazis. However, the guerrillas were grouped around two very different leaders: Tito, on the one hand, and Mihailović on the other. Tito's people received all kinds of support from the Russians, while the British supplied arms to Mihailović's people. After the war was over, the confrontation in Yugoslavia continued, but between the two guerrilla leaders, and when Tito emerged as the winner, he had his rival shot and thus achieved power. From this I draw the conclusion that the previous distribution of support by the Allied powers meant that it had to end like this, with Yugoslavia in the orbit of the Soviet or communist bloc, while the British ensured that they had Greece in their corner.

Photography and politicians

Although I have always thought of myself as a methodical, well-organised person with a great capacity for work, especially for my own work, which is what I like, I am well aware of my limitations. That is why I always say that I can only speak with a certain propriety and knowledge about photography, which is the thing to which I have dedicated my whole life. What I cannot talk about is politics or football, for example. But even if I cannot give my opinion on politics, I can say something about various politicians I have met or had dealings with through photography. When I was an assistant to the photographer Josep Sala, in my time with the Commissariat of Propaganda the Commissariat of Propaganda during the Civil War, we went to the Palau de la Generalitat to take a photograph of President Companys. Of course, I only carried the case with the equipment. We —I allow myself a small share of the credit— took a very good shot of the president that became the official photograph. Without knowing him, then, any more deeply than the fact of having seen him up close, and with the perspective of the years, I can say that, whatever mistakes or errors he made in his political career, he was a good person and a good president who should be forgiven any mistakes he may have made because he was prepared to sacrifice himself for the country. He was a martyr, a victim… and for that alone he deserves my forgiveness and that of the rest of the country, if there is anything that must be forgiven.

Among the other politicians I have met in the exercise of my profession were the mayor of Barcelona and the president of the Provincial Deputation of Barcelona, Porcioles and the Marqués de Castell-Florite, respectively. I met the latter when I was taking photographs for the magazine *San Jorge*, which was published by the Deputation itself, but I must confess that I only managed to get a sense of him as a very attentive person and little else.

I went to photograph Mayor Porcioles in his office in the
City Hall and dared to ask him if we could take a few more shots
on Montjuïc with the city in the background. He immediately
said yes. Even though people now say that he was a bad mayor and
that he destroyed the city, but I think that the mayor before him
was worse. I am referring to Simarro, who boasted in the pages
of *La Vanguardia* that during his term in office, not long after the
Civil War, the City Council had never declared a deficit but always
shown a profit. This cannot be! A city council is almost obliged to
have a deficit because this is a sign that it has been doing things
for the city and its citizens. Nobody remembers Simarro, but, in
contrast, everyone knows Porcioles. He did many things for the
city. Some bad? Maybe so. But he also had many successes. Or at
least that is my modest and sincere opinion.

Regarding the politicians that were closest to me, and were
important for the political activities of the country with the
restoration of democracy, I can think of a few with whom I had
some contact, although not a close involvement or friendship.
For example, regarding President Tarradellas, of whom I had
known when I was young, on one occasion I had to take some
photographs of him shortly after his return from exile. The first
thing he said when he saw me was ask if I was still living on Carrer
del Pi, which showed that he had recognised me and that he had
an extraordinary memory. When I was photographing him, he told
me he was hot and asked me to open the window, which I did.
A little later he decided there was a draft and asked me to close
it again, and then added: 'Forgive me for ordering you around,
but I enjoy it so much!' Some years later, when he was no longer
president, I went to see him again to take more photographs, and
on that occasion I was able to meet his wife, Antonieta, a very
charming and attentive person.

I had not previously met Tarradellas in person, of course, but
I had often heard my father speak well of him. I think that of all
the political figures of the time, he was the only one who could
be called a professional politician. He was also a great orator, one

of the few that I remember who never had to read his speech. However, I have to admit that I did not believe everything would go so well on the return of the president and the freedoms lost with Francoism, since I feared that with Franco's death and the end of the dictatorship we would be thrown into turmoil again… Fortunately, that did not happen and the democratic transition was managed very well. I am not a monarchist, but I recognise that King Juan Carlos was an important element in the peaceful transition, in that his role and his figure ensured that Francoists felt protected. In short, what really counts is that it all went very well and we did not find ourselves at war again.

As for the current president, Jordi Pujol, I recall going to the Palau to take a picture of him that was published on the front page of *La Vanguardia*. I have kept a picture of him as a souvenir, from the day he presented me with the Sant Jordi medal. If I say that Tarradellas was a true professional politician, what I will say about Pujol, because I believe it, is that he is a good shopkeeper. Now, I would not like this comment to be misinterpreted or taken as derogatory, quite the opposite, because I write them with admiration: he is a good shopkeeper. He does his job well, he fulfills his mission, which is to buy and sell for the good of the country. I have always voted for him and, what is more, I have a real affection for his wife, whom I have known since I was a child, when we were neighbours.

As for the mayor of Barcelona, Pasqual Maragall, I have photographed him several times, always at public events. However, I wanted to take different photographs of him, and one day I asked to meet at the Canaletes fountain, where I took a few shots, and we then walked down to Plaça Reial to finish the job. Maragall is a person I appreciate very much from both the personal and the political point of view. I remember that on one occasion, with his sense of curiosity and wanting to know about everything, he came to my studio to see how I work. I have also voted for him, because, for me, what counts is not so much the ideologies (I have never taken any interest in politics) as the way things are done. That

is why, when it comes to voting, I always decide at the very last
moment, when I am standing at the table with the voting papers. I
am always undecided, as I am before taking a photograph. There is
only one moment when I stop doubting: the moment I press the
button and it clicks.

On the subject of politicians and their ways of doing and
being, I remember a day when I was on Passeig de Gràcia, taking
photos of details of some of the façades. Suddenly I heard someone
approaching and saying: 'What is Català-Roca doing here at this
time of day?' The speaker was none other than the then Minister of
Defence, Narcís Serra. And I thought: How things have changed!
In the past, I had heard my father talk about the politicians of the
day, some of whom were his colleagues and friends, but I had never
actually met any of them until democracy arrived, when people
I had met and had dealt with in various ways –some of whom
were much younger than me– were placed in positions of political
responsibility.

IX.
My history of the image

Powerful image

Human beings have always felt the need to reproduce a figure, a character, an image, a landscape or a moment of the reality that surrounds them, whatever the form in which it is presented. A good example of what I am talking about is the famous Altamira caves in Santander. Think of a person who lived in the interior of the country in which they were born, and died without having ever left the place. Without a doubt, this person would have seen reality, but they would never have seen an exact representation of it. For this reason, I believe that the Church sought to attract these people, the inhabitants of a particular place, by building churches with a qwealth of paintings that would bring them closer to a concrete, real and imaginary world. Moreover, I am convinced that Romanesque murals were neither more nor less than what we now know as advertisements, so that looking at these paintings would lead people to believe in the idea of God in human form: just, approachable… In other words, churches and murals were both a means of conveying in comprehensible form what the Church wanted to say to its parishioners and advertising. Continuing in the same line, we can see that the artists were the ones that did most to immortalise the outstanding historical characters and events. For this reason, wealthy people had their portraits painted, in order to pass them down to posterity, and it is also why so many painters in the nineteenth century specialised in portraiture. However, when photography was invented, many of these artists switched to photography, but mostly those who were not really artists, since the really creative talents did wanted nothing to do with this new art. It was precisely at this time that the new isms emerged, such as Pointillism, Impressionism and so on, artistic movements in which colour was the dominant characteristic.

The latter part of the nineteenth century saw the invention of the offset press, thanks to which photographs could be reproduced, especially in the graphic arts. Later, with the advent of trichromy, photogravure artists were able to reproduce images in colour.

In my life I have spent a lot of time thinking about the how and why of images, and I have occasionally come to ponder sych curious questions as, for example, why Leonardo da Vinci's *Mona Lisa* should be so important and so well-known all over the world. What is so special about it that makes it stand out from the thousands of other works of art in the Musée du Louvre? Her enigmatic smile? Or could this intriguing answer be nothing more than a speculation made precisely to justify and explain the fact of its popularity? Honestly, I think the secret of the *Mona Lisa* is its small size and portability. Until the end of the nineteenth century, with the invention of the offset process for the transfer of photographs to the printed page, the accurate mass dissemination of works of art had not been possible. Successive improvements in the graphic arts would eventually allow the printing of colour plates, complicated and laborious though it was. So it was that when the first photo engravers had to choose a work to reproduce in colour, they chose a small picture that could easily be taken to the printworks. Successive generations of photo engravers did the same, and in this way the painting in question gradually gained in status, becoming an essential for any new publication in which it was referred to. And that is why it became so popular, because, without having ever seen the actual painting, everyone already knows it from its reproductions.

On photography

A good photograph is defined, in my opinion, by the fact that it is able to communicate well —very well— a situation, a person, a landscape… And to do so in such a way that it captures the interest of the person who sees it. And in this sense, we must agree that the result of a photograph must be the same as that of written narrative, of literature, since the situation that a photographer can convey are also images of real, everyday life or of fiction. The writer does it through writing, with words. A photographer, with the image. But since writing is much older, we know how to interpret it, because there are rules: grammar, syntax, spelling… And that is not yet the case in the field of photography, because there are no such rules. In other words, there is no organising grammar, although there are now great theorists in the world of the image, but ultimately, in my view, it is the people who will create and shape this process of ordering and interpreting photography. Because it is not just about seeing an image in the photograph. It is about —and this is what I like and what I aim to achieve— finding other things of interest in a photograph. Not just a face, a figure, a countenance, some trees…

Let me give an example: many years ago I took a photograph of the great American writer Hemingway in the bullring of Pamplona, during the San Fermin bullfights. In the foreground, we see the faces of the writer, a soldier and others. This would be the real image, the one you take in at first glance. But in this photograph there are more things, more details, if you learn, of course, reading, grammar. For example, Hemingway's eyes. He is looking down at what is happening in the square, at the bull and the bullfighter, of course. The soldier's gaze is fixed in the same direction, but a little less tightly focused; he is looking at the distance between the bull and the bullfighter. And the woman who is also in the photograph is looking in a different direction, the opposite direction, in fact: she does not like what she is seeing and her expression is one of disgust. What I like, then, is that when people look at my photographs they can see in them precisely this whole series of things I have just detailed, and that they go beyond the fact that this is a photograph of the famous American writer, which is what we perceive at first glance.

In this same line, one day a friend who was looking at a photograph of Miró from behind, contemplating some paintings, said he really likes my photo of Miró with wings. And it did look as if Miró had wings. For this reason, I believe that the language of photography, of the image in general, is far more universal and more understandable than any other, and is for everyone. In terms of the image, the greatest and most popular genius of this century is undoubtedly Charlie Chaplin. His films have been seen all over the world and by the most diverse audiences and absolutely everyone has understood them.

I have often been asked in interviews if I consider myself an artist, and I invariably reply that I think of myself as a natural observer, an observer of everything and everyone. I focus my attention on what interests me, what makes an impression on me, I open camera shutter and capture the reality of the moment. I believe that photography is more similar, or closer, to literature than to painting, quite the opposite of what is usually claimed. To make what I'm saying quite clear, I should add that you don't need a camera to take a photo. As I have said, I am an observer of human nature, and as such I am always looking, always observing. And I file everything I see in my head, as if my brain were a computer. Before I set to work with the camera, I already have a whole series of elements, references and data that help me do my job better and faster. Therefore, from my personal and always subjective —albeit very thoughtful— point of view, photography is a subtractive system in that what you do is take, capture; in contrast, painting is an additive system in that you start with a blank canvas, which you have to paint, you have to fill it. For this reason, I always say that I don't take photographs, I capture them; because the images are already there. Of course, you just have to be prepared to catch them at the right moment. That is also why you always have to know what you want to say and how you want to say it, as with literature. It is in this sense that photography must be understood as a distinct entity from the other arts; and, for this reason, I feel that I am a creator, not an artist.

There are other aspects of the photographic world, such as art photography, photojournalism… Personally, I am not interested in all these classifications. After all, what do 'art' and 'artistic' mean? They are just words used to define or label. I am only interested in one type of photography: the one I do. That plain and that simple. There are, of course, other ways of taking photographs, but they have nothing to do with me. For example, there was an exhibition of Mapplethorpe's work at the Fundació Joan Miró. I am not interested; I find it disgusting. He is a photographer who makes his photos, whereas I like to find the photo, as I was already doing long before Cartier-Bresson. Live! *LIFE*! I often see photographers tiring themselvres out taking photos, wasting roll after roll of film on the same person, event or news item. You see them firing off shots like crazy… Twenty, thirty shots! My son Andreu says it's like hunting rabbits with a machine gun. I only take two or three shots, because before I shoot I have to see the thing, if not there is no point shooting. Those avalanches of click-click-clicks are pointless, wasted efforts. I have a story that illustrates my way of thinking very well. There was a man who worked in a bank who used to boast about being an excellent marksman. Wherever he fixed his gaze, he put the bullet. One of his colleagues used to laugh at these claims to sharpshooting prowess, and the great hunter naturally wanted to prove that what he said was true, that his aim was superb. So, one Sunday they went out to Les Planes together. Our hunter placed a bottle at a considerable distance, took aim, fired… and missed. Of course, his colleague burst out laughing. 'What? Do you think this is easy?' our marksman said in response to the laughter. 'Let's see you try it.' His companion resisted for a while, but finally accepted the challenge. He took the gun with shaking hands, jerking the barrel to and fro, and fired. And hit the target! The great marksman scowled and said: 'Of course you had to hit it, aiming all over the place!' Well, all these photographers do the same. They point their cameras here, there and everywhere and sooner or later a good photograph will result from so many shots.

Something similar also happens in other fields. In cinema, for example, my other great passion. You very rarely see a really bad film, but there are not many great ones either. They don't make films like Chaplin's anymore. I don't even want to hear about directors such as Spielberg or Coppola… I have no interest in them, and I have no time for what they do.

I am also often asked if anyone can become a first-rate photographer, and my answer is always yes, if they are really dedicated and work hard. I know, immodest though it is to say so, that I am a good photographer. And I am a good photographer because I was raised on photography from infancy and because I have dedicated almost every hour of my now rather long life to it. What made Picasso, Miró and Dalí geniuses? Quite simply, because in addition to being innate geniuses they devoted their every waking hour to work. They dedicated themselves entirely to their work, to the craft of painting. I see many people who work, but very few who devote themselves utterly to their work. That is why I believe there is no need for specific rules or grand methodologies. I only believe in perseverance, hard work and the job well done. Photography must be lived and worked at.

As I have said on more than one occasion, I see the photograph before I take it. One of my best shots of New York, for example, I had already seen hours before I took it. I knew that I had to take it just before seven in the evening for it to be just as I saw it. And so I went there, I prepared everything and I waited until it was time to press the button.

I have also said that photography is a medium of communication. And to talk about photography, we have to talk about the other media that came before it. As everyone knows, the first form of communication was the gesture, which has the disadvantage that if the people who wish to communicate are not within sight of each other there is a total lack of communication, of course. We then realised that by making a guttural sound we could get the other person to look at us. These sounds were gradually enriched until we could converse with each other, although to reinforce spoken language, verbal communication, we still use gestures. Another system of communication evolved on a surface, as cave painting and hieroglyphics, which were the image of what a person wanted to convey to others, and this is how writing was invented.

The evolution of communication did not stop (in fact, it will never stop) and so, a century and a half ago, photography was invented. And, as I have said, photography is based on painting, which was the medium that most resembled it. So, it is natural that people should have begun by making portraits of great figures. Of Napoleon, for example, the only portraits we have are paintings, but there are photographs of his brother Jérôme. The first photographers emerged from the world of painting, because they were only mediocre painters. In the early years, photographic portraits were done with very much the same poses as those in painted portraits, with the disadvantage that they lacked colour.

If illiteracy has now all but disappeared thanks to the massive incorporation of children into the classroom to learn to read and write, history is repeating itself with the visual image, but with an important difference: it is not in school that children learn to see visual images. Instead, images are widely available to them in newspapers, illustrated books, films, television…

I feel sure that a day will come when, if you show someone a photograph, they will be able to tell you what time it was taken. In the half century that I have been actively involved in the world of photography and the visual image I have witnessed the great progress being made in this area. For example, about twenty-five years ago, I took a series of photos to illustrate a book about bullfighting, but the editor rejected some of them, the ones I had taken expressly to capture the movement. He excluded them on the grounds that they were moving, which goes to show that he did not understand the first thing about photography. Now, I am sure that this would not happen now, when so many photographs are taken with movement and people know how to understand them. For me, photography, as I think I have said, is a language through which the photographer speaks, and the viewer knows how to listen and understand. This being so, I regard writing and photography are two very closely related means of communication. If a writer describes a sunset well, the reader will see it, and if a photographer takes a good photograph of that sunset the viewer will see it in the same way and know how to interpret it.

What is the difference between the two procedures? Both start from looking at a piece of paper that connects directly to the brain; on one, however, the key signs are letters, syllables and words, and on the other the keys are the black or coloured inks. The difference between the two media, then, is minimal. That is why I believe that the two media are destined to collaborate: a text can be illustrated and a photograph can be described. And another significant fact or noteworthy feature of photography is the possibility of simultaneity. That is, the same exhibition can be held in different galleries and even in different countries at the same time. A clear example of this is *The Mediterranean Odyssey*, a collaborative project involving seven countries around the sea's shores, including Spain and Catalonia, which combined a design show and an exhibition of photographs and took place in six different cities at once: New York, Boston, Dallas, Philadelphia, Miami and Washington. And, of course, this is only possible with photography, because you can make as many prints from a photo as you want.

Needless to say, I, for one, am very happy to see the great advances that the world of photography is making with its coming of age.

The achromatics

Without leaving the field of photography, which is naturally the area I know best and in in which I feel very comfortable, there are matters about which I have always been concerned and to which I have sought to find a satisfactory response. This is true of what I call achromatics. Allow me to explain. Defining things in two words, such as black and white, does not make any sense —to me, at least— because, of course, there are always nuances in everything. In the case of black and white, it would be more correct to use the word 'achromatic' to define things without colour. I am almost certain that the new generations, those of the coming century, will define us in the twentieth century as achromatic, and rightly so, because this century has lived mostly in black and white. Painting and sculpture have always been polychrome, they have always used colour. For this reason, photography has had to incorporate colour into its natural language, since photographs are and must be able to be identified with reality. And reality is in colour!

Do we need to recall our history to remind us that colour has always been used? Books were written and drawn by hand and in colour, and the great door of Santa Maria monastery in Ripoll and the Parthenon in Athens (to give two very different examples in terms of culture and civilisation) were polychrome…

The passage of time, poor conservation, and the ravages of war (something we must not forget) have steadily erased these characteristic features, and the humanity has been lost. We have become accustomed to black and white, or to achromatism: we have had to make an effort of imagination and language to capture reality, to the point that we often use expressions such as 'sky blue', 'flesh tone' or 'earth colour' to visualise certain shades. With colour photography we no longer need to make that effort. I am convinced that one day we will even learn to recognise colour temperature, so that when we see a photograph, we will know what time it was taken and whether the light was natural or artificial. And we will arrive at all of this, I am quite sure, because black and white will have definitively disappeared.

In fact, if photography had always been in colour, no one would have missed black and white… An example of what I am saying is the fact that black and white weddings are gradually disappearing. I shall explain. I had always been curious about the fact that when a couple got married, the bride would be in white and the groom in black; and what could be the reason for

this behaviour if not the great persuasive power of the image? A
century or so ago, she would probably have worn a dress in a light
and cheerful shade of pink or blue and he a serious suit in brown
or navy blue. When the photographs were taken to immortalise the
important event, the result would lead future generations to believe
that she was wearing white and he was wearing black. And not
only with the images in the family album, but also with the photos
of a royal wedding and the newsreels and fictions of the incipient
cinema, this practice gradually became established. It can be said
that, from the eighties, when the automatic camera or home
video became widespread in homes, the tide turned, and colour
reappeared. By the way, at the last wedding I attended the bride
wore green.

Cinema

There were cinemas in Valls, of course, but my first contacts with
this world were at school. Sister Elvira had a small projector which
my father had sold her, and she would show us Felix the Cat films
and, from time to time, a film my father made when I was very
little of me with a rocking horse. This film has been lost. Later I
went to a cinema, the Apolo, to see a silent film called *Wings*, set in
the First World War; then *Ben-Hur*, the first version starring Ramon
Novarro, which was already starting to incorporate sound, but
not yet dialogue. I remember the construction of the Valls cinema,
designed by Cèsar Martinell, a *Modernista* architect who worked
with Gaudí. It was there that I saw the first sound film announced
(though I didn't see the film). In 1931, when we moved to
Barcelona, I noticed that some cinemas had a sign reading Sonoro,
which meant that the others were silent.

I used to go to the Bonsuccés cinema in the square of the
same name. It was silent and cost 25 cents for general admission
and 35 cents for the better seats. I would occasionally go to the
Capítol, popularly known as Can Pistoles, because they used to
show films with gunfights, but only rarely because it was much
more expensive, charging 75 cents.

Shortly before the war, the Maryland cinema opened, which during the Franco era was forced to change its foreign name and was called Plaza instead. Luckily for me, the manager was the father of my friend Pere Ardanuy, so I got tickets for all the premieres. There I was able to see and enjoy films such as *A Midsummer Night's Dream*, by Max Reinhardt, with James Cagney and Dick Powell; *Little Women*, with Katharine Hepburn; *Vanity Fair*; and many Paul Robeson films, in which he would sing while floating down the Mississippi.

The cinemas also showed productions by the German company UFA, which made very good films, from which I remember a very prominent leading couple, Marta Eggerth and Jan Kiepura, and the actress Anny Ondra, the wife of the German boxer Max Schmeling, who at that time came to Barcelona to fight Primo Carnera and Paulino Uzcudun. These fights were put on by three Central Europeans whose names were Strauss, Perlo and Lowman. These characters wanted to make themselves popular here so that the local politicians would let them install roulette tables in the casinos. The story was reported in the newspapers, and I remember seeing a photo of a roulette wheel in *La Vanguardia* in which the logo clearly embroidered on the baize was a composite of the first syllables of the three promoters' surnames. This gave rise to the word *estraperlo*, which during the war and post-war was used to refer to illegal business when it came to light that the famous *estraperlo* roulettes were rigged.

Shortly before the war I saw a film in a place at the far end of La Rambla and was much impressed by a girl in the cast. I wanted to know more and found out that she was called Margarita Cansino, and I was not far wrong in my favourable assessment: before long she changed her name to Rita Hayworth.

The cinema was a great catalyst for emotions. Whole families would go together, taking snacks and drinks, and loudly voice their delight, their disapproval, their fear… while the anonymity of the darkened theatre also made for a lot of fooling around and mischief. Things have changed a lot, and nowadays what I witnessed

at a screening of a film starring the Mexican singer Jorge Negrete
would be most unlikely: at the end of a musical number, which was
received with rapt attention, the applause and shouts of enthusiasm
went on for so long that the projectionist felt obliged to rewind the
reel and run the song again, just as they did in the zarzuela theatres.

Returning to cinema, from which I have strayed a little, in
recalling these curious characters I am reminded of *Carnival in
Flanders*. This was one of the films I saw most times, not because I
liked it so much but because, when the war broke out, the cinemas
ran out of new films and had to keep showing those they had. Even
then I was already highly critical of the photography of the films
I saw, and I remember that when I was especially interested in the
cinematographer who shot the film, this critical sense of mine was
heightened. For example, the cinematographer on quite a few of
Indio Fernández's films was Gabriel Figueroa. My friends would
recommend these films to me because they assumed that I would
like them, but in fact I didn't like them at all because, in my opinion,
the photography was bad. Figueroa frequently used a red filter that
made blue black, so the clouds contrasted dramatically with the
sky, and of course, that was too noticeable. I consider that good
photography should not call attention to itself. Only a photographer
should really be aware of it and know how to evaluate it, and the
ordinary spectator should not even notice it. The photography, I
insist, should not attract our attention, but should be part of the
larger whole. At thirteen, I was very well acquainted with all of Man
Ray's photographic work, but I didn't like it at all because it was
manipulated. I remember, however, that in the early years of cinema,
someone invented a camera lens that compressed the image on the
film stock, and so another lens had to be used to widen it when it
was projected. When television arrived and started to compete with
cinema, the film studios started to use this invention, CinemaScope,
so that audiences would appreciate the difference in size and format
over television. The inventor, as is often the case, had already died.
But, of course, to screen an old film shot in an earlier format, the reel
had to be trimmed at the top and bottom to follow the panoramic

fashion. I was perfectly aware of all this, of course, because I could read the image, but most people only knew how to read books, not visual images. In this sense, it is like reading a book with the top and bottom lines of each page cut off. Now, when Néstor Almendros won the Oscar for Best Cinematographer, I went to see the film, but since the cinema showed it trimmed the top and bottom, I couldn't watch it and had to walk out. I have never heard anyone else comment on the cut. When I saw Abel Gance's *Napoléon*, it was far ahead of its time, because it was shot with three cameras to achieve a panoramic effect. In the cinemas, however, they screened it in three narrow cuts! My heart sank, but no one complained. And when Francis Ford Coppola restored it, with music by his father Carmine, I was one of those who felt that he should not have done that, because he completely distorted Gance's cinematic vision… The arrival of colour cinema constituted another stage in the struggle between the big screen and television, since the latter was still in black and white (for a short time, at least). Cinema managed to revive itself a little, but it seems that television has supplanted cinema in terms of the mass audience.

On one of the many trips around Spain on which I took the photographs for the Ministry of Information and Tourism's posters, I stopped in Pastrana, in Castilla-La Mancha. At the inn where I was staying, I was told there would be a film show that evening and that the only requirement for attendance was to take a chair to sit on. Loving the cinema as I did, I was there in no time, as the saying goes. I have no recollection of the film I saw, but I do recall that the next day I was riding out of town on my scooter to my next location and had already gone a few kilometres when I spotted a gypsy caravan with a sign that said Cine Sonoro, and seeing the sign, I stopped. A Roma woman came over to me and asked where I was from. When I told her Pastrana, she said that was where they were going, to put on a film show. Of course, I informed her that there had been a film show there the night before, to which her blunt response was: 'I don't give a shit about the priests.' The priests and the Roma competed with one another in the screening of films. But the funniest and most surprising thing was what she said next. When I asked what they were going to show, she said 'Colas' –'tails'. I said I didn't know what that was, and she explained that there was a man in Madrid who bought cuts –discarded film footage– and spliced them together. The whole thing struck me as quite fantastical! A surreal montage seasoned with a large dose of magical realism, offering the people of the rural towns and villages a glimpse of an utterly alien, unknown reality which they would otherwise never have seen.

I say realism because I happen to believe that, when sound films were invented, cinema was destroyed, because it happened in an illogical manner. In my opinion, the logical thing would have been for sound films to have come before silent films, and silent films before photography, rather than the other way around as actually happened. I say this because people were already long accustomed to the theatre, that is, to action and speech, so the most logical thing would have been for what they already knew to be invented, namely sound film. The next logical step should have been silent film, because cinema without words would have been readily understood all over the world, so there would have been no need for dubbed versions or subtitles. And, following this logic, the last step should have been the invention of photography: the snapshot freezing the most sublime moment. Of course, I cannot deny that these reflections are not overwhelmingly logical. I must admit, and perhaps I should have started from here, that I have a particular interest in silent film, more than anything else because it deprived the director of the possibilities of using speech, so that in creating images they had to delve deeper, in a more rigorous exercise of imagination. In short, silent film was much richer. But I also happen to believe that this impediment will also be overcome. There is currently a Euronews television programme called *No Comment* which only shows footage of the most important events of the day, and I think that in a few years it will all be like this again. Words will not be needed to communicate our everyday reality. Images will be quite sufficient.

Chronology

1922: Francesc Català i Roca, son of photographer Pere Català i Pic, wis born in Valls on 19 March.

1931: He moves to Barcelona with his family, where Pere Català i Pic combines advertising and industrial photography with his work as a theorist and educator.

1935: He receives his professional training within the family, helping his father in the morning and in the afternoon studying at the Acadèmia Cots on Portal de l'Àngel. He begins to study drawing at the Llotja Escola de Belles Arts.

1936: He works with his father on an assignment to photograph Paul Éluard. Català i Pic's relations with ADLAN and GATCPAC introduce the young photographer into avant-garde cultural circles.

1937: He begins to work at the Generalitat de Catalunya's Commissariat of Propaganda, where his father was director of publications during the Civil War.

1939: He resumes his drawing studies at Llotja.

1941: He resumes his photographic activity with his father, focusing on industrial photography and the reproduction of paintings.

1948: He becomes independent from his father and opens his own studio. From this point on, he combines his work as a professional photographer with research and the investigation of new techniques. He wins the Fundador poster prize.

1950: Two of his photographs are awarded prizes by the magazine *Populart fotographic*. He wins the Ciutat de Barcelona photography award with the series 'Octubre'.

1951: He begins his involvement with the magazine *Revista*, providing the photographs for Cesáreo Rodríguez Aguilera's reports. He meets Salvador Dalí. He is awarded the Ciutat de Barcelona photography award for the second time and the Ciutat de Barcelona cinema award for his first film, *La ciudad Condal en otoño*.

1952: He wins the City of Barcelona cinema award *ex aequo* with the film *Piedras vivas*, which is subsequently awarded first prize at the Ancona

Film Festival. He takes part in the first Grup R exhibition at the Galeries Laietanes and continue to do so until the group is dissolved in 1959. His friendship with Joan Miró begins with his work with film director Thomas Bouchard. *La Sagrada Família* marks the start of his long career in publishing books of photo-essays.

1953: At his first individual exhibition, in the Sala Caralt in Barcelona, he shows his photographs in greatly enlarged prints, without a mount or glass, which becomes his habitual practice from then on.

1954: He begins a long-running association with the Destino publishing house, providing the photographs for numerous of tourist guides with texts by Luis Romero, Josep Pla, Alexandre Cirici, Gómez de la Serna, Rafael Alberti, Gabriel Celaya and Néstor Luján, among others.

1958: He is commissioned to create large photographic panels for the World's Fair in Brussels.

1959: He is commissioned by the Dirección General de Turismo to take photographs of tourist destinations all over Spain. He takes advantage of these trips to take his own photographs. He begins to use colour slides. He exhibits a selection of his tourist photographs at the Sala Neblé in Madrid.

1965: He begins his researches into colour.

1966: The Col·legi d'Arquitectes de Barcelona presents the exhibition *Les cases parentals*.

1967: He resumes his activity as a filmmaker with a series of reports for TVE. He receives the Medalla y Placa al Mérito Turístico from Manuel Fraga.

1970: Commissioned by Aimée Maeght, he begins to make documentaries about various visual artists: Miró, Chillida, Guinovart. He travels to Japan with Joan Miró.
From these years are the films: Miró-Artigas; Mural de ceràmica de Joan Miró, and *Miró-Osaka, 1970. Peinture Murale.*

1973: A project for the Blume publishing house marks the beginning of his travels in the Americas. He definitively abandons black and white behind photography. He makes the film *Teles cremades*, on the creation of the series of this name by Joan Miró.

1976: He makes a film about the painter Guinovart's exhibition *Contorn. Entorn* at the Galeria Maeght.

1977: Three new films: *Chillida ceramista, Peine del viento* and *Femme/ Woman. A Tapestry by Joan Miró.*

1978: He shoots the film *Miró - La Claca* about the play *Mori el Merma*, a collaboration between the puppet theatre group La Claca and Joan Miró.

1980: His film *Femme/Woman. A Tapestry by Joan Miró* about the tapestry in Washington, D.C. receives the Golden Eagle award. He begins to work with the newspaper *La Vanguardia* and the magazine *Gaceta Ilustrada*.

1982: First retrospective exhibition at the Galeria Maeght in Barcelona with the title Francesc Català-Roca. Photographs. Artists. Architects. Characters. Bulls.

1983: He presents an exhibition of photographs about Joan Miró at the Galeria Maeght. He exhibits at the Agrupació Fotogràfica de Catalunya. He is awarded the Premio Nacional de Artes Plásticas by the Ministry of Culture.

1984: The travelling exhibition *Personajes de los años 50* is presented at the Biblioteca Nacional in Madrid. Exhibition of photographs by Joan Miró at the Galeria Quatre Gats in Mallorca and in Bogotá. The exhibition *Tauromaquia* is presented at the Museu Picasso in Barcelona.

1986: He exhibits at the Galeria Ferran Cano in Mallorca.

1987: The retrospective exhibition *Francesc Català-Roca. Photographs* is presented at The Spanish Institute in New York. He films a report on the reconstruction of Mies van der Rohe's Barcelona Pavilion. His exhibition *L'arquitectura dels anys 50 a Barcelona* is presented at the Col·legi d'Arquitectes de Catalunya in Barcelona.

1988: The Institut d'Estudis Vallencs in Valls puts on an exhibition of his photographs of Gaudí's work.

1989· He exhibits at the Col·legi d'Enginyers Industrials de Catalunya in Barcelona.

1990: The Galeria Maeght in Barcelona hosts the exhibition *Francesc Català-Roca. Del meu arxiu.*

1991: He exhibits at the Sonimag 1991 trade fair in Barcelona.

1992: The Generalitat de Catalunya awards him the Premi Nacional d'Arts Plàstiques and presents him with the Creu de Sant Jordi medal. His hometown of Valls awards him the Títol d'Honor.

1993: Gold Medal for Artistic Merit, from the Barcelona City Council. Exhibition *Mirar Miró* at La Pedrera. The Fundació Joan Miró in Barcelona presents him with the Ocell Solar award.

1994: The Department of Industry and Energy of the Generalitat of Catalonia awards him the title of Master Artisan.

1995: Can Sisteré in Santa Coloma de Gramenet hosts the exhibition *Generacions*. He exhibits at the Espai Guinovart in Agramunt. At the suggestion of J. M. Castellet, he writes his memoir *Impressions d'un Fotògraf.*

Filmography

La ciudad Condal en otoño
1951. 16 mm film. Sound. Black and white. 20'.
Production and cinematography: F. Català-Roca.

Piedras vivas .
1952. 16 mm film. Sound. Black and white. 20'.
Production, cinematography and direction: F. Català-Roca.

Artigas. Céramique
1969. 16 mm film. Sound. Colour. 23'.
Production: Aimé Maeght.
Cinematography: F. Català-Roca.
Music: Jean-Pierre Finkbeiner.

Miró-Artigas
1970. 16 mm film. Sound. Colour. 11' 40".
Production: Aimé Maeght.
Cinematography: F. Català-Roca.
Music: Jean-Pierre Finkbeiner.
Director: F. Català-Roca.

Miró Osaka. 1970. Peinture murale
1970. 16 mm film. Sound. Colour. 13' 17".
Production: Aimé Maeght.
Cinematography and direction: F. Català-Roca.
Music: Jean-Pierre Finkbeiner.

Miró 73. Toiles brûlées
1973. 16 mm film. Sound. Colour. 19' 53".
Production: Aimé Maeght.
Cinematography and direction: F. Català-Roca.

Mural de ceràmica de Joan Miró
1975. 16 mm film. Sound. Colour. 12' 45".
Production: IBM Barcelona.
Cinematography and direction: F. Català-Roca.

Contorn. Entorn
1976. 16 mm film. Sound. Colour.
Production: Aimé Maeght.
Cinematography and direction: F. Català-Roca.

Peine del viento
1977. 16 mm film. Sound. Colour.
Production: Aimé Maeght.
Cinematography and direction: F. Català-Roca.

Chillida ceramista
1977. 16 mm film. Sound. Colour.
Production: Aimé Maeght.
Cinematography and direction: F. Català-Roca.

Femme / Woman. A Tapestry by Joan Miró
1977. 16 mm film. Sound. Colour. 25'.
Production: National Gallery of Art, Washington, D.C.
Cinematography and direction: F. Català-Roca.

Mori el Merma / Miró - La Claca
1978. 16 mm film. Sound. Colour. 30'.
Production, cinematography and direction: F. Català-Roca.

Mies van der Rohe. Barcelona 1929
1987. 16 mm film. Sound. Colour.
Production: Fundació Pública del Pavelló Alemany de Barcelona de Mies
van der Rohe.
Cinematography and direction: F. Català-Roca.

Bibliography

Antonio Machado en Baeza. Text: Cesáreo Rodríguez Aguilera.
Photographs: F. Català-Roca. A. P. Editor, Barcelona, 1967.

Arquitectura de Sert en la Fundació Joan Miró. Text: Bruno Zevi. Photographs:
F. Català-Roca. Ed. Polígrafa S.A., Barcelona, 1977.

Arquitectura moderna a Barcelona. Text: David Mackay. Photographs:
F. Català-Roca. Edicions 62, Barcelona, 1989.

Arte Ibérico. Text: M. Tarradell. Photographs: F. Català-Roca. Ed. Polígrafa
S.A., Barcelona, 1969.

Arte paleocristiano. Text: Pedro de Palol. Photographs: F. Català-Roca.
Ed. Polígrafa S.A., Barcelona, 1979.

Arte Romano en España. Text: M. Tarradell. Photographs: F. Català-Roca.
Ed. Polígrafa S.A., Barcelona, 1969.

Artesanía popular de América. Texts: various authors. Photographs: F. Català-
Roca. Ed. Blume, Barcelona, 1979.

Artesanía popular española. Text: M. A. Pelauzy. Photographs: F. Català-
Roca. Ed. Blume, Barcelona, 1977.

Artesanía popular mexicana. Text: Carlos Espejel. Photographs: F. Català-
Roca. Ed. Blume, Barcelona, 1977.

Barcelona. La conquista de espacio. Arquitectura (1980-1992). Text: Joan Barril.
Photographs: F. Català-Roca. Ed. Polígrafa S.A., Barcelona, 1992.

Barcelona. Text: Luis Romero. Photographs: F. Català-Roca. Ed. Barna, 1954.

Cerámica popular española. Text: J. Llorens Artigas and J. Corredor Matheos.
Photographs: F. Català-Roca. Editorial Blume, Barcelona, 1970.

Chillida. Catalogue of the exhibition at the Carnegie Museum of Art.
Photographs: F. Català-Roca. Maeght Editeurs, París, 1979.

Chillida. Text: Peter Seiz and James Johnson Sweeney. Photographs:
F. Català-Roca. Ed. Abrams, New York, 1986.

Clavé escultor. Text: Lluís Permanyer. Photographs: F. Català-Roca.
Ed. Polígrafa S.A., Barcelona, 1988.

Clavé. Text: Pierre Seghers. Photographs: F. Català-Roca. Ed. Polígrafa
S.A., Barcelona, 1971.

Costa Brava. Text: Luis Romero. Photographs: F. Català-Roca. Ediciones CID, Barcelona, 1958.

El moble català. Text: Josep Mainar. Photographs: F. Català-Roca. Ed. Destino, Barcelona, 1976.

El parlament de Catalunya. Texts: Jaume Sobrequés, Francesc Vicens and Ismael E. Pitarch. Photographs: F. Català-Roca. Publicacions del Parlament de Catalunya, Barcelona, 1987.

El Parlamento de Cataluña. Texts: Jaume Sobrequés, Francesc Vicens and Ismael E. Pitarch. Photographs: F. Català-Roca. Publicacions del Parlament de Catalunya, Barcelona, 1981.

El pavelló alemany de Barcelona Mies van der Rohe. Texts: various authors. Photographs: F. Català-Roca. Fundació Pública del Pavelló Alemany de Barcelona Mies van der Rohe, 1986.

El Pirineu. Text: Estanislau Torres. Photographs: F. Català-Roca. Ed. Destino, Barcelona, 1970.

El que hem menjat. Text: Josep Pla. Photographs: F. Català-Roca. Ed. Destino, Barcelona, 1981.

Els monestirs catalans. Text: Antoni Pladevall. Photographs: F. Català-Roca. Ed. Destino, Barcelona, 1968.

Esgrafiats de Picasso. Text: Alexandre Cirici. Photographs: F. Català-Roca. Col·legi Oficial d'Arquitectes de Catalunya i Balears, Barcelona, 1965.

España. Text: M. A. Pelauzy. Photographs: F. Català-Roca. Ed. Blume, Barcelona, 1977.

Folk Art of the Americas. Texts: various authors. Photographs: F. Català-Roca. Ed. Abrams, New York, 1981.

Fotografías acromáticas. Photographs: F. Català-Roca. Tibidabo Ediciones, Barcelona, 1995.

Gargallo i Barcelona. Text: Alexandre Cirici. Photographs: F. Català-Roca. Ed. Ariel, Barcelona, 1974.

Gaudí. Text: Ignasi de Solà-Morales. Photographs: F. Català-Roca. Ed. Polígrafa S.A., Barcelona, 1983.

Guía de Castilla la Nueva. Text: Gaspar Gómez de la Serna. Photographs: F. Català-Roca. Ed. Destino, Barcelona, 1964.

Guía de Cataluña. Text: Josep Pla. Photographs: F. Català-Roca. Ed. Destino, Barcelona, 1961.

Guía de Cuenca y principales itinerarios de su provincia. Text: César González Ruano. Photographs: F. Català-Roca. Ed. Planeta, Barcelona, 1955.

Guía de Madrid. Text: Juan Antonio Cabezas. Photographs: F. Català-Roca. Ed. Destino, Barcelona, 1959.

Guía de Murcia. Text: José Vicente Mateo. Photographs: F. Català-Roca.
    Ed. Destino, Barcelona, 1971.

Història de l'art català. Texts: various authors. Photographs: F. Català-Roca.
    9 vols. Edicions 62, Barcelona, 1985-95.

Joan Miró i Catalunya. Text: Joan Perucho. Photographs: F. Català-Roca.
    Ed. Polígrafa S.A., Barcelona, 1969.

La arquitectura de los años cincuenta en Barcelona. Photographs: F. Català-
    Roca. MOPU, Madrid, 1987.

La caza de la perdiz roja. Text: Miguel Delibes. Photographs: F. Català-
    Roca. Ed. Destino, Barcelona, 1988.

La Costa Brava. Text: Josep Pla. Photographs: F. Català-Roca. Ed. Destino,
    Barcelona, 1978.

La fiesta del arroz. Text: Vicens Esteve. Photographs: F. Català-Roca.
    Gacitol S.A., Barcelona, 1994.

La presència de Joan Prats. Text: Alexandre Cirici. Photographs: F. Català.
    Ed. Polígrafa S.A., Barcelona, 1976.

La Sagrada Família. Text: Cèsar Martinell. Photographs: F. Català-Roca.
    Barcelona, 1952.

Les cases pairals catalanes. Text: J. de Camps i Arboix. Photographs:
    F. Català-Roca. Ed. Destino, Barcelona, 1965.

Libro del mar. Poems by Rafael Alberti. Photographs: F. Català-Roca.
    Ed. Lumen, Barcelona, 1968.

Llorens Artigas. Text: Francesc Miralles. Photographs: F. Català-Roca and
    Martí Català. Ed. Polígrafa S.A., Barcelona, 1992.

Llorens Artigas. Text: Pierre Courthion. Photographs: F. Català-Roca.
    Ed. Polígrafa S.A., Barcelona, 1977.

Los campanarios de España. Text: Santiago Alcolea. Photographs: F. Català-
    Roca. Barcelona, 1972.

Los espacios de Chillida. Text: Gabriel Celaya. Photographs: F. Català-Roca.
    Ed. Polígrafa S.A., Barcelona, 1974.

Mallorca, Menorca e Ibiza. Text: Josep Pla. Photographs: F. Català-Roca.
    Ed. Destino, Barcelona, 1962.

Miró, noranta anys. Text: Lluís Permanyer. Photographs: Català-Roca.
    Edicions 62, Barcelona, 1984.

Miró escultor. Text: Jacques Dupin. Photographs: F. Català-Roca.
    Ed. Polígrafa S.A., Barcelona, 1972.

Miró sculptures. Text: Alain Jouffrey and Joan Teixidor. Maeght Editeur.
    París, 1973.

Miró & Artigas. Ceràmiques. Text: José Pierre and J. Corredor Matheos.
    Photographs: F. Català-Roca. Maeght Editeurs, París, 1974.

Personajes de los años cincuenta. Texts: Lluís Permanyer and Joan
Fontcuberta. Ministerio de Cultura, Madrid, 1984.

Santa Maria del Mar. Catedral de la Ribera. Text: Francesc Tort i Mitjans.
Photographs: F. Català-Roca, Martí and Andreu Català Pedersen.
Fundació Uriach, 1938. Barcelona, 1990.

Tauromaquia. Text: Néstor Luján. Photographs: F. Català-Roca. Ed. Nauta,
Barcelona, 1968.

Valls, capital de l'Alt Camp. Text and photographs: F. Català-Roca.
Ed. Destino, Barcelona, 1992.

Veure Barcelona. Text: Pere Calders. Photographs: F. Català-Roca.
Ed. Destino, Barcelona, 1984.

Veure Mallorca, Menorca, Eivissa. Text: Valentí Puig. Photographs: Francesc
Català-Roca. Ed. Destino, Barcelona, 1986.

Vieira de Silva. Text: J. Cassaigore-Weelen. Photographs: F. Català-Roca.
Ed. Polígrafa S.A., Barcelona, 1979.

Vuit segles de carrers de Barcelona. Text: Josep M. Espinàs. Photographs:
F. Català-Roca. Ed. Destino, Barcelona, 1974.

Sumari